```
786.3041 McL    200602
McLain.
Class piano.
```

**The Lorette Wilmot Library**
**Nazareth College of Rochester**

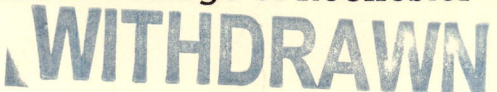

★ **Class Piano**

MARGARET STARR MCLAIN

# CLASS PIANO

INDIANA UNIVERSITY PRESS

Bloomington & London

## ★ Dedication

*To the many students who have tested these materials
and who have been, over the years,
my best teachers.*

200602

Published in 1974 by Indiana University Press
All rights reserved
Copyright © 1969 by Margaret McLain Hall

No part of this book may be reproduced or utilized in any form
or by any means, electronic or mechanical, including photocopying
and recording, or by any information storage and retrieval system,
without permission in writing from the publisher. The Association
of American University Presses Resolution on Permissions constitutes
the only exception to this prohibition.

Manufactured in the United States of America

**Library of Congress Cataloging in Publication Data**

McLain, Margaret Starr.
   Class piano.

   Reprint of the 1969 ed. published by Allyn and Bacon, Boston.
   1. Piano—Methods—Group instruction. I. Title.
[MT222.M15   1974]    786.3'04'1    73-19659
ISBN 0-253-31357-0

2  3  4  5  6  82  81  80  79  78

# Preface

In the belief that every music student, whatever his major field of study, should have a modicum of keyboard facility, many conservatories and schools or colleges of music require that all students receive piano instruction. While such a project is educationally desirable it presents economic problems. One solution is to provide class instruction in instruments other than the student's major instrument. In addition to the obvious savings in time, money, and the use of studio space, there are other advantages to this plan. Students gain satisfaction and encouragement from the opportunity to measure themselves against their peer group; an atmosphere of healthy competition spurs them on; they learn to play before one another; and they establish a foundation for ensemble playing.

As the physical and psychological circumstances of class instruction differ from those of private instruction, so also do its aims — particularly in college situations where course content must be tailored to the needs of degree-oriented students, many of whom are majoring in music education. In the case of piano skills these special aims have come to be expressed collectively by the term **functional piano,** which simply means "useful piano."

In functional piano the student learns to sight-read simple piano pieces, accompaniments, and vocal scores; he learns to transpose, play by ear, harmonize melodies, improvise an accompaniment, and modulate; he understands the underlying principles of good fingering, pedaling, and touch; he is at home in all keys and can apply at the keyboard the knowledge of chords and their uses which he has gained in his theory class. And, hopefully, he acquires sufficient digital dexterity to handle all these useful matters fluently and musically.

Most private teachers would agree that such skills are a desirable part of any pianist's equipment. Preoccupied with the individual pupil's repertory, style, and technic needs, however, few teachers have time or inclination to include strictly "functional" items in the private lesson.

Since the objectives of what might be called "artist pianism" and functional piano are dissimilar, it follows that much of the material used and the manner of using it must also be dissimilar.

In determining the suitability of materials for class instruction two requirements are of the utmost importance: 1) everything should be playable by the class as a whole (hence the duets, the limited-range drills, and the avoidance of multiple-choice solutions in chord progressions), and 2) everything should be capable of being fragmented, or reduced, to its smallest and most basic components so that it may be presented, comprehended, and mastered in easy and logical steps. To ignore the first requirement means something less than total class participation, which not only wastes time but may invite disciplinary problems. To neglect the second requirement will result in uneven or delayed progress by the class as a whole — the bright students taking several steps at a bound while the slower ones hesitate, befogged. For these reasons, with the exception of improvisation and the more advanced solos, everything in the book has been planned for performance by the class as a whole.

Two things which all college music students have in common are: 1) some prior knowledge of music, however rudimentary, or else they would not have been admitted to a conservatory or college of music, and 2) greater-than-average demands upon their time, because, in addition to the usual academic and professional subjects such students must put in long hours practicing instruments and voice. So, these considerations also have a bearing on the choice of materials and their use.

In the first instance the student has a distinct advantage: he already knows how to read music — at least a little; he understands note values and time signatures; often he has had some training on another instrument and sometimes he has attained a high degree of proficiency on that instrument. Every bit of this knowledge can be utilized, and means that the student, although approaching a new instrument, is not obliged to begin at the very beginning musically.

The second circumstance — limitation of time — means that the greatest possible benefit must be derived from every class and practice activity. It is not enough for a five-finger exercise to help the student gain finger independence; it must also be used to teach him half steps and whole steps and how to recognize them rapidly in all keys; it must teach him the difference between major and minor modes; it can give him the feel of the perfect fifth, so essential when not looking at the keys is a "must"; it can lay the groundwork for triads, seventh chords, and scales; and it will give the student something which he can soon harmonize either by himself or with his piano partner — thus gaining experience in two-hand coordination and ensemble. This is what is meant by *multiple purpose drills* and this principle has guided the author in the construction of all the drills, or *warmups* as they are called in this book.

During the past twelve years, piano classes at Boston University have varied in size from three to thirty students and have been conducted in rooms equipped with from one to twelve pianos. Many texts have been used; but while each was admirable in its way, none was found to meet all the requirements as outlined above. Those books which were primarily keyboard-harmony—oriented were only practicable in small classes where the instructor could give individual attention to the individual student in working out the assignments. Those collections or methods consisting mainly of carefully graded pieces and exercises were generally not adaptable to more than one player at a keyboard. Other texts, assuming no prior knowledge on the part of the student, began with the most elementary information, thus necessitating a somewhat pointless review or a plunge into the mid-portion of the text. Very little of this material could be made to serve more than the one ostensible purpose for which it was designed.

Thus came into being the present volume. The methods of presentation, as well as the materials, have been tested and retested. They are the result of trial and error, of discard and revision, and of proven practicability—*in large classes*. For it is axiomatic that what may be taught to a large class may equally well be taught to a small class, but that what may be taught to a small class is not always successfully taught to a large class.

So much for overview. In the Introduction are set forth the structural plan of the book, and suggestions for adapting it to specific class needs and teacher preferences.

## ✶ Acknowledgments

To my colleague, Dr. Eileen McMillan, I wish to express my grateful thanks for her valuable suggestions and criticism; to my daughter-in-law, Mrs. Eleanor Hall, appreciation for help in translating from the original German to English the words of the Mozart *Lullaby*; and finally, indebtedness to my husband, Whitney Hall, without whose cheerful stoicism in the face of neglect and added burdens this book could not have been written.

# Contents

**Preface**   v

**Introduction**   xv

**1.** Prerequisites   1

    Half Steps and Whole Steps

    Sight-Reading

    One-hand Melodies

    Transposition

    Playing by Ear

    Hand Gymnastics

    Rhythm Drill

    How to Practice

    Hearsay and Other Ear Work

    Review and Suggested Assignments

**2.** Major Triads   14

    Framing Chords

    The Dominant Seventh Chord

    Harmonizing Melodies

    Sight-Reading

    A Two-hand Melody

    Rhythm Drill

    Improvisation

Hearsay and Other Ear Work

　　　Review and Suggested Assignments

**3.** The Basic Principles of Fingering　　　　　　　　　　　　**24**

　　　Framing Chords from Above

　　　First Use of the Damper Pedal

　　　The Subdominant Triad

　　　Legato and Staccato

　　　Hand Gymnastics

　　　Rhythm Drill

　　　Sight-Reading

　　　Improvisation

　　　Hearsay and Other Ear Work

　　　Review and Suggested Assignments

**4.** Minor Mode　　　　　　　　　　　　**40**

　　　Octaves

　　　Names of Octaves

　　　Hand Gymnastics

　　　Harmonizing Warmups

　　　Sight-Reading

　　　Four Solos

　　　Rhythm Drill

　　　Improvisation

　　　Hearsay and Other Ear Work

　　　Review and Suggested Assignments

**5.** Major Scales in Tetrachords　　　　　　　　　　　　**60**

　　　Scale-Degree Names

　　　Change-Ringing — and Playing

The Circle of Keys

Harmonizing Each Degree of the Scale

Three Melodies to Harmonize and Transpose

Rhythm Drill

Non-Harmonic Tones

Sight-Reading

Improvisation

Hearsay and Other Ear Work

Review and Suggested Assignments

**6.** Minor Scales in Tetrachords — **80**

Major and Minor Scale Structure

Transposing the Minor Melodies in Chapter 4

Roots

Major and Minor Thirds

Triads in Three Positions

Rule for Finding the Root of a Chord

Common Tones

The Dominant Triad

Cadences

Intervals

Accompaniment Patterns

Some Basic Principles of Interpretation

Sight-Reading

Improvisation

Hearsay and Other Ear Work

Review and Suggested Assignments

**7.** Standard Scale Fingering — **110**

Strumming

Songs for Strumming

More Left-hand Accompaniments

Inversions

Modulating Up One Half Step

Rhythm Drill

Some Basic Principles of Pedaling

Sight-Reading

Improvisation

Hearsay and Other Ear Work

Review and Suggested Assignments

**8.** Diatonic Scales with Standard Fingering, continued — **146**

Arpeggios

Secondary Triads

Songs to Harmonize and Transpose

*Secondo* Accompaniments

Sight-Reading

Improvisation

Hearsay and Other Ear Work

Review and Suggested Assignments

**9.** Diatonic Scales with Standard Fingering, concluded — **177**

Chromatic Scale Fingering

Whole-tone Scale Fingering

Seventh Chords

Fingering for Seventh Chord Arpeggios

Improvisation

Hearsay and Other Ear Work

Review and Suggested Assignments

**10.** Legato Thirds and Chords                    **212**

    Embellishments

    Introductions

    Songs to Harmonize

    Playing Accompaniments

    Improvising for Activities

    Hearsay and Other Ear Work

    Review and Suggested Assignments

**11.** Artificial Rhythms                          **236**

    New Types of Accompaniment

    Improvisation

    Memorizing

    Hearsay and Other Ear Work

    Review and Suggested Assignments

# Appendix                                          **262**

    Three Little Words—Note, Key, and Tone    262

    Scale Chart    264

    Songs, Melodies, and Repertory
    (*in chronological order*)    268

    Songs and Melodies to Harmonize and Transpose
    (*in alphabetical order*)    272

    Repertory (*in alphabetical order*)    275

# Index                                             **277**

# Introduction

This book is divided into chapters, each of which generally will include elements of theory, harmonization of melodies, transposition, technique, ear work, sight-reading, improvisation, rhythm drills, duets, solos, review questions, and suggested assignments. Thus the student's knowledge and skill in several essential areas will be advanced simultaneously. Many of these elements could be omitted or the order changed. For example, improvisation might be deemed unnecessary; memorizing could be introduced at any point; and students should be encouraged to refer to the section on embellishments from the first appearance of a grace note.

The substance of each chapter can be covered in from three to six class meetings (five is average)—depending on such variables as size of class, number of pianos in room, aptitude of pupils, length of lesson periods, and homogeneity of class.

The author has been guided by certain basic philosophical concepts, foremost of which is the belief that students should be made to think for themselves as soon as possible, and to have confidence in and take responsibility for their own musical decisions when these decisions are based on sound principles. Correlative is the conviction that what is best remembered and assimilated by a student is what he has worked out—"discovered"—for himself rather than what has come via teacher-talk. Thus, once the fundamental principles of fingering are presented, the student is asked to determine, write in, and adhere to his own choice of fingering. Naturally, this is not accomplished without much time-consuming class discussion, experimentation, and challenge. Often, though not always, it is desirable for the class to use uniform fingering, but the teacher who achieves this by directive rather than by class choice is abridging a valuable element in the educational process.

For the same reason, expression and pedal marks have been omitted from much of the music and should be supplied by the student after experimentation and comparison. Editing, or absence of editing, in music by the earlier masters has been carefully preserved.

The three chief components of sight-reading—keyboard feel, reading ahead, and note-group recognition—are dealt with at an early stage. (The more complex phases of chordal structure and analysis, and of hearing the music mentally before it is played, are left to a period when the pianist has gained greater skill.)

Obviously, any sight-reading materials included in this volume will not provide true sight-reading because every normal student will browse ahead, thus familiarizing himself with what, to be of value, should be *un*familiar. The materials are intended, rather, to illustrate useful approaches to sight-reading and should be used first in this way—examining the music for key and time signatures and changes, chordal or scale-wise patterns of notes and their direction, similarities or variations in phrases or patterns, rhythms, ledger-line notes, repeats or *da capos*, page turns, and so on—all this before hand touches keyboard. The sight-reading exercises frequently incorporate the harmonic or technical topics currently being studied. At a later date they may be used for transposition and as models for improvisation.

Technique *per se* has been limited to certain fundamental exercises. Since there are many divergent opinions, each teacher will wish to state his own preferences as to hand position, finger action, pressure touch, and the rest. He may well wish to introduce supplementary technical work; but, if he does not, the warmups practiced in all keys will establish a reliable technical foundation while developing keyboard familiarity.

When scales are first introduced they are not considered in relation to technique, but rather as an essential part of good musicianship. This is the reason for the tetrachord presentation, which permits the student—with eight fingers over eight keys—to perceive the scale as an organic whole rather than as a series of isolated pitches. Many a pianist can play scales with flashing virtuosity but is at a loss when asked to play from dictation a simple diatonic sequence.

The Rhythm Drills are designed not only to develop understanding of rhythm but to develop two-hand coordination—an area which many students find most vexing—and later to aid hand-foot coordination in preparation for syncopated pedaling.

The melodies which the student is first given to harmonize and play by ear are familiar ones, capable of being harmonized by the simplest and most frequently used chords. As his harmonic vocabulary and pianistic resources increase, the student can return to these early songs with greater sophistication of harmony and accompaniment.

Although the theoretical elements of the text are designed to parallel and reinforce the usual college freshman theory and harmony courses, primary chords are first introduced by rote so that they may be put to immediate and satisfying use. Since theory is only part of the total spectrum of pianism, it has not seemed necessary to belabor it. However, should the book be used in a situation where collateral theory courses are not available—as in private teaching—it will be found to provide ample explanation.

Perhaps the most serious deficiency among music students is their lack of what one might call "listening skills." Many are unable to identify intervals, simple chords and their inversions, major and minor modes, the movement of a bass line, or various meters. From the very beginning such hearing-awareness is stressed and stimulated, for without it a student cannot hope to "play by ear" or improvise.

The repertory includes a number of vintage items which, though having served many generations, are fresh and useful to each new group of students and enjoyed by them. A wide range of difficulty and styles will permit the teacher to use those compositions best suited to the class needs and to make additional assignments to students with superior capacities.

Finally, although this text is self-contained, it is not intended for "do-it-yourselfers." Much could be learned by the student attempting to teach himself, but in the final analysis a teacher to correct, guide, encourage, and demonstrate is the pupil's best friend.

★ **Class Piano**

# ✳ 1 ✳

## Prerequisites

The fact that you are about to use this text means that you are one of the many persons with some musical knowledge but little or no keyboard skill. You probably are familiar with the names of the keys on the keyboard and very likely you have an understanding of time and meter, notation, key signatures, and clef symbols. If at any time an unfamiliar term appears here and is not immediately explained, be sure to look it up in your theory book or a music dictionary.

## Half Steps and Whole Steps

Piano proficiency involves many diverse elements which range from the strictly physical (finger agility and hand-eye-foot coordination) to the esthetic (tone, pedaling, interpretation) and the intellectual (improvisation, transposition, analytical listening), but for the beginner the first requirement is familiarity with the keyboard. This means more than a mere awareness of regularly spaced white keys punctuated by alternating groups of two and three black keys; it means a knowledge of **intervals,** and we shall begin with the smallest — **half steps** — because half steps are our building blocks and from the very start we must know how to use them.

Strike any white key on the piano keyboard. Now strike its nearest neighbor above, or to the right. The distance, or interval, between these two is a half step. Strike the key a half step below, or to the left of, the first key. One, or perhaps both, of these neighboring keys will be black. Try this on several other white keys, in each case locating the key a half step above and the key a half step below. Now start from a black key. You will notice that the neighboring keys are *white*.

Thus, half steps may occur between two white keys, or a black key and a white key, but not between two black keys.

**Chromatic scales.** When we have an extended series of half steps moving in one direction, we call it a **chromatic scale.**

Before playing a chromatic scale, let us number our fingers. The thumbs of each hand are designated "1"; the index fingers are "2"; the middle fingers, "3"; the ring fingers, "4"; and the little fingers, "5." This is unlike fingering for several other instruments, so beware of confusion.

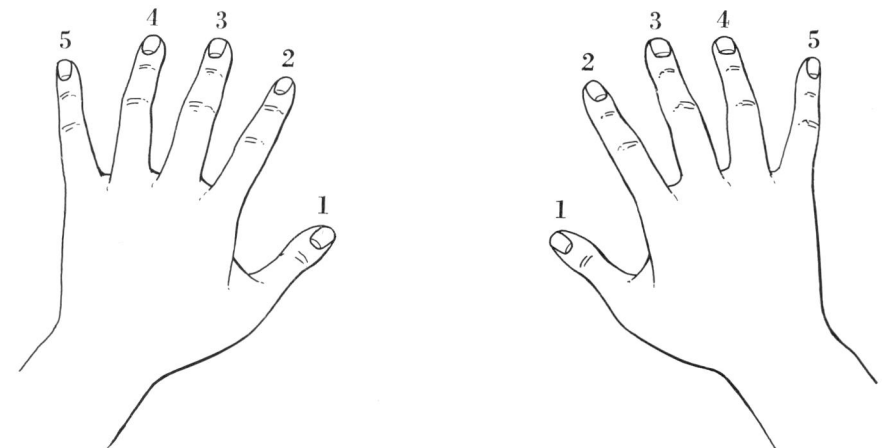

*Figure* 1.

Now, if you will put your right first finger—1—on **middle C** (the C nearest the keyhole or maker's name) and place 2, 3, 4, and 5 on each successive half-step above it, you will have a short chromatic scale.

*Figure* 2.

Play this up and down several times to get the feel of it. Play chromatic passages in other locations, starting sometimes on white keys and sometimes on black keys. Play Figure 2 with your left hand, beginning with the fifth finger and continuing with 4, 3, 2, 1. Do this several times, starting on both white and black keys.

**Whole-tone scales.** As you might suppose, two half steps make a **whole step.** Can you point to the keys one whole step up and one whole step down from B, F, A♭, G, C, D♯, and E?

Whole steps are sometimes called **whole tones,** and when we have an extended series of them we call it a **whole-tone scale.**

2  CLASS PIANO

Let us begin with the first finger of the right hand on a black key—
G♭. Can you discover the four whole-tone steps which climb from G♭?

*Figure 3.*

Play the same series with your left hand, beginning with the fifth finger. Construct other whole-tone sequences starting on black keys and on white keys, playing them with each hand, up and down.

**Diatonic scales and five-finger positions.** **Diatonic scales** consist of a combination of whole steps and half steps. When you place the fingers of your right hand over the five white keys from C to G, your fingers are on the first five tones, or **degrees,** of the C major scale. This is called a **five-finger position.** Play these keys one after another and as you do so notice whether they are separated by a whole step or a half step. If you found only one half step—between the third and fourth degrees—you were correct.

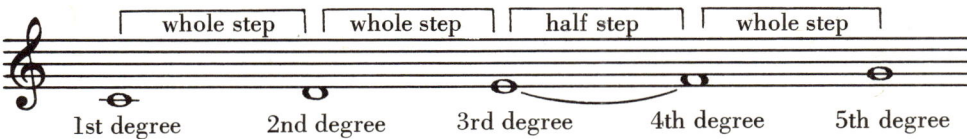

*Figure 4.*

Now you have the pattern for **all major five-finger positions:**

>   From 1 to 2 is a whole step
>
>   From 2 to 3 is a whole step
>
>   From 3 to 4 is a half step
>
>   From 4 to 5 is a whole step

This is expressed as follows:

>   1  2  3 ‿ 4  5

*Figure 5.*

With this knowledge and your familiarity with half steps and whole steps you can now play five-finger positions in any major key. Close your eyes and drop your right thumb at random on any key; then (having opened your eyes) construct a five-finger position on that key. Do likewise with your left hand, starting to play upward, of course, from the fifth finger. After you have experimented a bit more with these isolated five-finger positions you will be ready to organize them into our first **warmup.**

You will notice that in Warmup I each five-finger pattern is three measures long and ends with the same note on which it began. The ending note is a half note having two counts. This with the half rest gives you an entire measure in which to figure out the notes to include in the new five-finger position. Here are the first few sequences. When you have grasped the rhythmic pattern, carry the sequence through the entire octave—or farther, if you wish.

Two admonitions before you begin:

a. Play with curved fingers. (The nails should never come in contact with the keys, so keep them short.)

b. Be careful to play **legato,** which means *connecting* all notes. The tones should have no break between them, but neither should they overlap. Try to achieve a smooth, even effect from the outset.

### WARMUP I

At first, play this warmup hands separately. When you can do that easily, play it hands together, the left hand playing an octave below the right hand. Saying the scale-degree numbers aloud as you play will help you to establish the half step between 3 and 4 in each five-finger position.

## Sight-Reading

The ability to read and play music at sight is an essential part of any musician's equipment. Naturally, you must be completely familiar with the keyboard and the printed notes. If you are not, or if you can identify the notes readily in one clef but not in the other, you should make a careful study of the Grand Staff in your music dictionary.

In addition to instant note identification are three other factors of equal importance. First is **keyboard sense** or the "feel" of the keyboard, which enables your hands to find their way over the keys without your having to look. Without this ability the pianist is obliged to glance back and forth from the printed page to his hands, invariably losing his place in the music as well as on the keyboard, slowing the entire process, and inviting "stumbles." To play without looking at your hands may at first seem quite impossible but by following the directions in this book you will gradually develop skill.

The second ingredient essential to good sight-reading is the ability to *look ahead*. The very best sight-readers are able to look half a page ahead, as evidenced by the point at which they nod for the page to be turned. At the other extreme, the inept reader can scarcely wrench his eyes away from the note he has just played in order to examine the note he is about to play. As with keyboard sense, the ability to look ahead is a skill which can be developed and toward which we shall aim from the outset.

The third requirement is simply to *keep going*. Never stop to correct a mistake; leave out notes rather than impede the rhythmical progress of the music.

Counting aloud will help. Incidentally, it is a great advantage to establish a habit of counting at the very beginning of piano study, before time and rhythms become complicated and present problems.

These first exercises in sight-reading are merely note-key-identification—but with a difference: while you are playing one note you must be *looking* at the next! To help you do this make a **sight-reading pacer** by cutting a strip of cardboard 5 or 6 inches long by 1½ inches wide. Hold one end of it with your left hand while you play the notes with your right hand. This is how it works:

1. Look carefully at the clef sign, the key signature, and the time signature.
2. Look at the first note.
3. Cover the note with the pacer, held horizontally, then play the note with your right hand, counting the required number of counts in an even, moderate tempo, and at the same time *looking* at the second note.
4. On the next count of "one" play the second note, at the same time covering it with the pacer. *Look* at the third note.
5. Continue in this way, always playing and covering a note simultaneously, and *looking* at the next note to be played.

For this exercise you may use any finger which is convenient. You may sometimes have to glance down at the keys since you have not yet developed keyboard sense. Playing the notes with the left hand and using the pacer with the right hand is a trifle awkward but entirely possible. Two players at one piano may take turns "pacing" each other. Later, when sight-reading involves playing with two hands, help from another person can be of the greatest benefit.

These and all subsequent sight-reading exercises should be played three times.

### SIGHT-READING FOR THE RIGHT HAND

### SIGHT-READING FOR THE LEFT HAND

## One-hand Melodies

Now that you have mastered five-finger positions and have made a start at sight-reading, you are ready for some "pieces," but just melodies for the present.

*Lightly Row* consists of only the tones in one five-finger position. Examine it carefully, identifying the highest and lowest notes, then decide which five-finger position your hand should cover. Next, determine which finger should strike the first note and mark the finger number in pencil over that note. Do the same with the left hand, locating the five-finger position, then marking the correct finger number over the first note.

Before playing *Lightly Row* on the piano, play it "in the air" with each hand alone, at the same time singing the scale-degree numbers. Do not confuse the scale-degree numbers with finger numbers even though they are the same at the moment. They will correspond only briefly with your right hand finger numbers and almost never with your left hand numbers.

Follow the same procedure with *Oats and Beans*, determining which five-finger position will accommodate all the notes of the song and marking the appropriate fingering over the first note. Again, play each hand in the air before playing on the piano.

LIGHTLY ROW

German Folksong

## OATS AND BEANS

Singing Ga

## Transposition

**Transposition** means playing music in a key other than that in which the music is written. If you are transposing to a key with the same letter name as the original key—to A major from A♭ major, for example—you have only to substitute a different signature (three sharps in place of four flats) while reading the same note-letter on the staff. The A♭ then becomes A♯ but is still located in the second space of the treble staff. Figure 6 will make this clear.

*Figure* 6.

If you were transposing F♯ major into F major you would substitute one flat for the six sharps but still find F in the first space of the treble staff. In other words, you *imagine* a different key signature but continue to *read* the notes as you see them printed on the staff.

Now play *Lightly Row* in the key of C♯ major (imagine a sharp before each of the notes) and in the key of C♭ major (imagine a flat before each of the notes). Play *Oats and Beans* in the key of A major (see Figure 6). Even if you are not sure of all these signatures you will still be able to transpose the songs if you have constructed the five-finger positions correctly.

The process is different when the letter name of the new key is not the same. In this case you must transpose by means of scale-degree numbers. While your melodies are restricted to the first five degrees of the scale this is very simple. Here are the steps you will follow:

1. Notice which scale degree the song begins on.
2. Sing the scale-degree numbers of the song in the original key.
   In *Lightly Row* you would sing 533−|422−|1234|555−| etc.

(The dash after a number signifies that that tone is held longer.)

3. Place your hand over the five-finger position of your new key, being sure that each finger is on the correct key. (Check the whole steps and half steps.)
4. Sing and play the song in the new key, starting with the same scale degree that you began with in the original key. Thus, if you began with the fifth degree in the original key, you will begin with the fifth degree in any other key.

## Playing by Ear

The expression "playing by ear" often connotes a species of fumbling, hit-or-miss-and-mostly-miss gropings at the keyboard which is rightly condemned by serious musicians. Playing by ear need not, however, be of this order. When undertaken with informed awareness it can be useful and pleasurable. It is merely a matter of *knowing* what one has heard, or is hearing in the mind's ear, and reproducing it. "Knowing" is the key word; guessing has no place in this scheme, nor has luck. As you progress in your studies you will be given many opportunities to develop the necessary discriminating and analytical ear.

Everyone is familiar with *Merrily We Roll Along* (or *Mary Had a Little Lamb*) so we will begin with that.

1. Sing or hum the tune to make sure you recall it.
2. Select a five-finger position in a range which is comfortable for your singing voice. Play the five notes up and down slowly.
3. Decide which of these tones the melody begins on. Try to do this without testing on the piano, although you may sing or hum as much as you wish.
4. The first tone of the song, and its place in the five-finger position, will naturally determine which finger should play first.
5. Using scale-degree numbers, sing and play the song without a mistake.

Follow the same procedure for *Hot Cross Buns*. For this song you will not need all the notes in your five-finger position so decide how many you will need and which degrees they are. Then determine the fingering.

Play each of these songs "by ear," hands separately, and in several keys.

An amusing auxiliary game is to try to identify by scale degree, when away from the piano, the first notes of various songs which come to mind or which one hears on the radio. Not all songs begin with a tone in the five-finger position, but when they do, the first tone should be easily identifiable after a little practice.

## Hand Gymnastics

In the early stages of piano playing, many a student experiences difficulty in making his hand do his bidding and in coordinating his two hands. The Hand Gymnastics will help you gain mastery over the various parts of your hand, and the Rhythm Drills will help with hand coordination as well as with rhythm.

### I

*Starting position.* Forearm and hand upright, fingers and thumb pointing to ceiling.

*Second position.* Bend wrist and extend hand straight out, at right angle to forearm.

*Third position.* Straighten hand up to starting position.

*Fourth position.* Extend fingers straight out, at right angle to palm.

*Fifth position.* Straighten fingers up to starting position.

*Sixth position.* Bend first and second joints of fingers as far as possible. Try to press finger tips against edge of palm.

*Seventh position.* Straighten out to starting position.

*Eighth position.* Spread fingers. Shake hand loosely.

## Rhythm Drill

With the right hand, play the upper line of notes on one key of the piano while tapping the lower row with the left hand. Then play the lower row and tap the upper row. Now reverse the process, playing the upper line with the *left* hand and tapping the lower line with the right hand, then tapping the upper line with the left hand and playing the lower line with the right hand. Be sure that the taps are loud enough to hear.

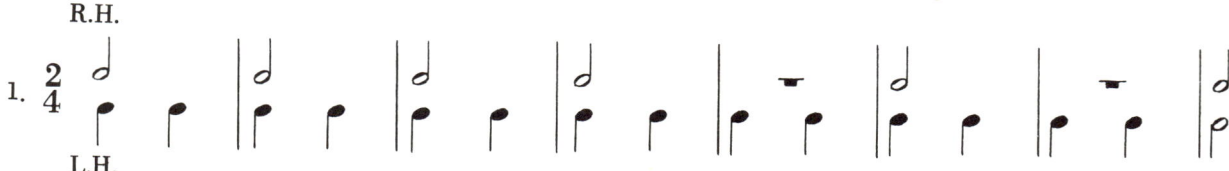

10  CLASS PIANO

Make up and write down similar rhythm drills.

## How to Practice

The final words in this chapter concern practice. No matter how elementary the level at which you begin, the way in which you practice is of the utmost importance. First of all, regularity is essential: a half hour each day is better than three hours once a week. Next, have a plan. The plan may vary from person to person depending on degree of advancement, amount of time devoted to practice, and individual needs, but the following precepts can guide you:

1. Tackle first whatever is most difficult.
2. Do not devote a disproportionate amount of time to any one segment of the assignment.
3. Arrange the several items in your assignment so that they will provide variety in your practice period.
4. Save for the end that which you find most enjoyable.
5. At each practice period, while specific needs are fresh in your mind, make a plan for the next practice period. This will insure continuity and minimize practice by whim or chance.

## ⋆ Hearsay and Other Ear Work

1. Identify (by ear) chromatic, whole-tone, and diatonic five-finger positions as the teacher plays them.
2. Identify isolated half steps and whole steps.
3. Identify individual scale degrees in five-finger positions which have been played for you.
4. Play a note on the keyboard (within your vocal range) and *sing* a half step higher, a whole step higher, a half step lower, a whole step lower.
5. Play *Merrily We Roll Along* and *Hot Cross Buns* by ear in every major five-finger position, singing the numbers of the scale degrees.
6. Identify by scale degree (within a five-finger position) the first tone of different familiar melodies which the teacher will play.
7. Write out *Merrily We Roll Along* and *Hot Cross Buns* leaving a blank staff below the melody where chords may be written in later. Choose any key except C.
8. Make up and write down six rhythm drills using different meters but restricting yourself to note and rest units of whole, dotted half, half, and quarter values.

## ⋆ Review and Suggested Assignments

1. Define the following terms and symbols. If any are unfamiliar check them in your theory text or a music dictionary.

    Interval; octave; scale; middle C; measure; half note; half rest; sequence; range; 𝄞; $\frac{4}{4}$; ×; ♭; ♮; ♯; 𝄢; ♭♭; clef; Grand Staff; key signature; time signature; diatonic scale; whole-tone scale; five-finger position; double bar; half step; whole step; scale degree; chromatic; transpose.

2. Locate keys a half step above and a half step below every key in one octave.
3. Locate keys a whole tone above and a whole tone below each key in one octave.
4. Name the white keys in one octave.
5. Give two names for each black key in one octave.
6. With your eyes closed, play Warmup I through all major keys, hands separately, then hands together.

7. Indicate how the fingers of each hand are numbered.
8. Play *Lightly Row* in major five-finger positions on each key in an octave. Do this hands separately, singing the scale-degree numbers as you play. After you have played it while watching your hand, play it again in the same key with your eyes closed. Play *Oats and Beans* in the same way.

# ✶ 2 ✶

## Major Triads

If you place your hand over any five-finger position and strike the first, third, and fifth keys simultaneously you will have played a **chord.** Chords are of several kinds. This one is a **major triad.** Play major triads on D♭, F♯, B, E♭, G, A♭, C♯, B♭, and E.

The word "triad" means "three notes," and because these triads are constructed on the first degree of the scale they are called **I chords,** or **tonic triads.** Play them hands separately, then hands together, one octave apart.

We can now expand our first warmup into the following:

WARMUP II

You will notice that the successive tones of the five-finger position are written as eighth notes and therefore move twice as fast as the quarter notes in Warmup I.

Play this warmup through all keys, hands separately, then hands together, if you can.

## Framing Chords

In Western music the interval of the **fifth** (1 to 5) is important for many reasons, but the reason which immediately concerns us is that it is useful in helping to establish "keyboard feel," mentioned before in connection with sight-reading.

With your right hand, play a C major triad. Now, without letting your fingers deviate in the slightest, lift your hand high above the keyboard—two or three feet—then bring it down on the same C major triad and see if you have been able to maintain the exact triad position. Do the same with the triads on G and on F. Now try it with your left hand on the same keys. When you have mastered this, practice on the triads of D, A, E, and B majors. One or two black keys will change the "topography" of the triad a bit. After this, build triads on the black keys and try to hold your exact triad position as your hand travels up and down. This is called **framing a chord** and will be of great use to you, for by fixing the precise shape and sensation of the triad in your "hand's memory" you are mastering not only the feel of the fifth but of the **third** (1 to 3, or 3 to 5) as well.

## The Dominant Seventh Chord

Anyone who has studied theory or harmony will readily identify the pedigree of our next chord. For our present purpose, however, it is best approached by rote. It is a **dominant seventh chord,** indicated by the symbol $V_7$ and found as follows: play a G major triad with your right hand; now move the lowest **voice,** or **part** (played by your thumb), down a half step from G to F♯; move the middle voice up a half step to C; retain the highest tone—the fifth. Strike the F♯, C, and D together using your 1st, 4th, and 5th fingers, and you will have just played a $V_7$ chord.

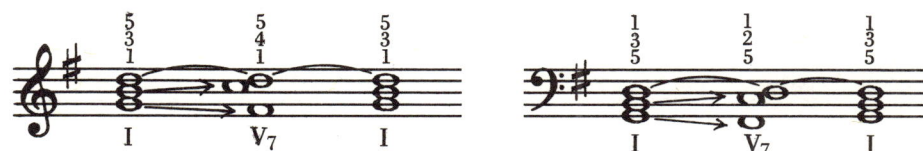

*Figure 7.*

When you play the chord with your left hand you will finger it with 5, 2, 1. Because it is a **dissonant** chord you will generally want to follow it with a tonic triad, or in technical language, **resolve** it.

Play the I $V_7$ I pattern in all major keys, first hands separately, then hands together.

## Harmonizing Melodies

When you can play the I $V_7$ I pattern easily in any key you are ready to harmonize the songs you learned in Chapter 1. All of them can be harmonized with the two chords in your repertory but you will want to do some experimenting to determine which chord sounds best where. In general, a chord sounds best on a strong beat, especially if the chord introduces a change in harmony, but you do not have to limit your chording to strong beats, nor do you have to alternate your two chords. After you have tested several harmonizations, indicate in the music the one you think best by writing the chord symbol (I or $V_7$) in pencil under the appropriate note.

Once you have decided on the harmonization, you may perform the piece in several ways. You can play the melody with the right hand and the chords with the left hand, or you can play the melody with the left hand and the chords with the right hand. Or two players can make a duet of it, the lower player striking chords with both hands while the upper pianist plays the melody with hands an octave apart. This could be reversed too, the upper player chording and the lower player providing the melody. Another version would be to play the first phrase one way and the second phrase another way. Can you think of other possibilities?

Here are two more melodies to be harmonized with I and $V_7$. Play the melody with each hand, first in the air, then on the keyboard, harmonizing with the other hand. After you have mastered the songs in the keys given, transpose them to all other keys.

### SLEEP, BABY, SLEEP

German Lulla

### ROSA

Flemish Folksong

(For additional songs to play, see *Hearsay and Other Ear Work* in this and the following chapters.)

## Sight-Reading

In this chapter's sight-reading you will proceed as before, playing with one hand and covering up the measure about to be played with your pacer, only now you will sometimes be asked to observe and retain in your mind's eye *two* notes since the pacer will always cover an entire measure. Again, note carefully the clef, key signature, time signature, and contents of first measures. Once you have begun playing, the important things to watch for are **direction** (progression of notes up or down), and whether the notes move **stepwise** or **chordwise.** For example, you should be able to recognize immediately that the notes in Figure 8 progress upward and in a stepwise pattern, while the notes in Figure 9 move downward and chordwise.

*Figure* 8.                                                                 *Figure* 9.

Even if you are not sure of the identity of some of the notes, recognizing that a series of notes is proceeding stepwise from a note which you do know will help you to find them. (By "step-wise" we mean, of course, in a series of neighboring scale degrees.)

In the same way, recognizing that notes *skip* one or more lines or spaces will indicate that these are chord-tones. While this can become more complicated because of the greater variety of intervals involved, you are not likely to find in the simple music which now occupies you any melodic intervals other than those of the chords with which you are familiar.

*Do not forget to count out loud!*

## A Two-hand Melody

In this melody the left hand plays the notes with stems turned down, the right hand plays those with stems turned up. Do not harmonize or transpose.

THEME FROM FINALE OF NINTH SYMPHONY

Beethoven
1770–1827

Here is your first two-hand piece. The melody falls into a five-finger position and the chords are the familiar I and $V_7$. You can transpose it quite easily.

## LYRIC PIECE NO. I

H. Hollins Banberry
1936–

## WARMUP III

This warmup is for finger independence. Depress the triad *silently* and hold it down while repeatedly striking the 2nd and 4th fingers. Then hold down the 2nd and 4th fingers while repeating the triad. Some of the held-down fingers may want to come up and you may have to help hold them in place with your free hand.

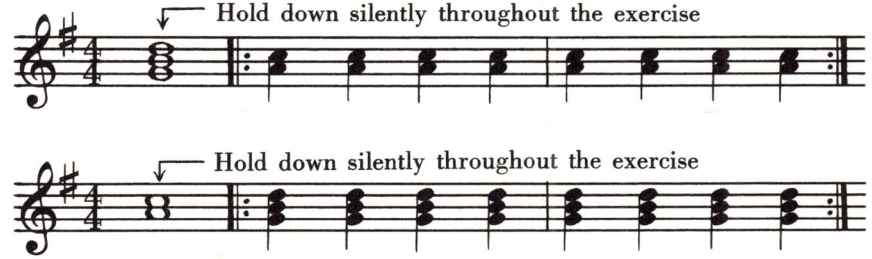

## Rhythm Drill

Play and tap the rhythm drills as directed in Chapter I.

CHAPTER TWO

## Improvisation

At one time the ability to **improvise,** or **extemporize,** was considered an essential part of the equipment of any keyboard virtuoso, and his public performances often included demonstrations of his skill. This seldom is done today; but if it is becoming a lost art on the glamour circuit, it is becoming increasingly needful in functional music. Most modern and interpretive dance is accompanied by improvised music; children in kindergarten and primary grades have all manner of activities which are coupled with and dependent upon improvised music; improvisation has long been a part of progressive jazz and Dixieland, and recently composers in more sedate circles have been experimenting with group improvisation.

Despite this last circumstance, improvisation is not suited to large-class activity although it can be handled to advantage in small classes. In any case, practice is essential. Even if you have no creative talent, you can still learn to improvise.

Unlike composition, which permits the student to test alternatives, reconsider, and improve, improvisation is subject to absolute time limitations. Once begun, the music must continue without interruption to the end; there must be no stops to correct false notes and harmonic crudities. To consider all the elements involved—harmony, melody, rhythm, fingering, interpretation, variety, change of key, mode, form—is to realize that this is no small task. Since the first necessity is to "keep going" you should begin by using only the simplest materials.

**Rhythmic improvisation.**   1. Clap two measures in $\frac{4}{4}$ time. Use quarter note and half note values, and dotted rhythms if you wish. A pattern such as Figure 10 is not too simple.

*Figure* 10.

The important thing is to complete the planned number of measures, to know where you are in each measure, and to keep a steady tempo.

2. Invent and clap three or four more two-measure sequences in $\frac{4}{4}$ time.

3. Clap several two-measure sequences in $\frac{3}{4}$ time and in $\frac{6}{8}$ time.

4. Clap several four-measure phrases in $\frac{4}{4}$, $\frac{3}{4}$, and $\frac{6}{8}$ time. Again, the most important consideration is to clap the designated number of measures. If you wish, you may try irregular phrases of five or six measures, but you must know at all times which measure you are in, and you must complete the phrase with the number of measures projected. Do not attempt complicated rhythms.

5. Using a I chord in any key, play a rhythmic series of four measures as in Figure 11.

*Figure* 11.

Improvise different rhythmic phrases on different triads, hands separately. Do this in various meters.

**Melodic improvisation.**   With each hand alone, make up rhythmic phrases using the triad tones individually as in Figure 12. Again, do this in different keys and meters.

*Figure* 12.

**Two-hand improvisation.** 1. Play a tonic chord in the bass at the beginning of each measure to accompany a triad-tone melody in the right hand.

*Figure* 13.

2. When you can manage four measures easily, improvise eight-measure periods of two phrases each as suggested by Figure 14 and Figure 15.

*Figure* 14.

*Figure* 15.

3. Play chords with the right hand, melody with the left hand, as in Figure 15.

You will observe that in Figures 14 and 15 the second phrase is almost exactly like the first phrase. This is not a requirement, but it is a simple and frequently used way of providing structural balance. If the last note of the first phrase is a tone other than the tonic, and the last note of the second phrase *is* the tonic, a kind of question-and-answer effect results. The device can be modified so that only the beginning of each phrase is alike.

For the improviser, this technique has the merit of making one idea do the work of two.

### ⋆ Hearsay and Other Ear Work

1. By ear identify isolated chords as major triads or dominant seventh chords as they are played for you.
2. From a given pitch in your voice range sing the three tones of a I chord, the three tones of a $V_7$, and again the tones of the I chord, singing from the bottom up. Sing tones of the same chords from the highest down.
3. Play the chorus of *Jingle Bells* by ear, following the instructions given for *Merrily We Roll Along;* then harmonize it in all keys.

### ⋆ Review and Suggested Assignments

1. Define the following terms or symbols:
    triad; ♪; tonic; resolve; stem (of note); slur; head (of note); flag; dissonant; beam; dot; ⌢ ; >; simile.
2. Play Warmup III in all major keys, hands separately.
3. With each hand frame major triads on black keys and white keys, and in low, middle, and high locations on the keyboard.
4. Frame $V_7$ chords in the same way.
5. With eyes closed play I $V_7$ I in all major keys, hands separately, then together.
6. Determine which of your two chords sounds best with each note of a five-finger position.
7. Play Warmup II with one hand and harmonize it with the other. First play it slowly, harmonizing each eighth note, then play it faster, harmonizing only the first and third counts.
8. In the empty staves which you provided when you wrote *Merrily We Roll Along* and *Hot Cross Buns* in Chapter 1, you may now write the proper harmony.

# ✶ 3 ✶

## The Basic Principles of Fingering

Most melodies exceed the five-finger-position range so devices must be employed to enable the hand, or hands, to move smoothly and securely over the entire keyboard. If you understand the basic principles of good **fingering** you will be able to work out that which is best suited to your individual hand and not be dependent on another person's guidance, or on the finger indications in the printed music, which are not always best for your particular needs.

In an earlier era it was considered undesirable to use the thumb on a black key if this could possibly be avoided. You will see evidence of this in most older editions of standard works. Today, more and more pianists are concluding that the thumb on a black key is frequently the simplest and smoothest solution to certain passages.

Figure 16.

Here are the principal fingering devices:

Extension:

*Figure* 17.

Contraction:

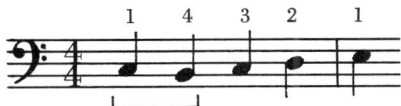

*Figure* 18.

Replacement:

*Figure* 19.

Passing fingers over the thumb:

*Figure* 20.

Passing the thumb under the hand:

*Figure* 21.

Lifting the hand to a new location (hand shift):

*Figure* 22.

Changing fingers on a repeated note:

*Figure* 23.

Changing fingers on a sustained note (organ fingering):

*Figure* 24.

"Gliding" from one key to its neighbor with the same finger:

*Figure* 25.

Although some of these examples are written for the right hand and some for the left, they are applicable to either hand.

Experiment freely with all of the devices. Occasionally some of them will overlap as when a **contraction** or **replacement** becomes, in effect, a **hand shift.**

Sometimes only one fingering is feasible; at other times several will be acceptable. There also will be passages for which *no* comfortable solution seems possible and you must settle for the least awkward. In every case test several fingerings before you decide on the best one, then *mark it in your music and stay with it!* It is most important to use exactly the same fingering each time you play a passage in order to establish a habit, or "conditioned reflex." Failure to do this results in timidity, insecurity, and stumbling. None of this applies to music intended solely for sight-reading, where any preparation would rob it of its newness and thus of its value.

In most educational music, fingering is indicated only where it is necessary to depart from a five-finger position or standard scale or arpeggio fingering. Also, when fingering is indicated for a special passage it is seldom indicated on repetition of that passage. When this happens, mark the fingering in yourself to insure against fingering the passage differently each time.

Do not mark fingering for each note on the printed page. Mark only a departure from the natural finger sequence; when every note has a number above it the eye has difficulty identifying which number is important and which is not. There is also some danger of becoming a finger-number reader instead of a note reader.

FRÈRE JACQUES
(A Round)

French Folksong

This song can be harmonized in two ways: you can play a I chord on the first count of each measure, or you can play a I chord on the first count, a $V_7$ on the second, and a I on the third.

After you have played the song as a duet and as a hands-together harmonized solo, play it as a **round.** To do this, the first player begins alone. At the third measure the second player starts from the beginning, playing an octave or two lower or higher. Players continue to enter this musical game at two-measure intervals for as long as there are players and pianos. It ends when the last player has been through the piece four times.

Since this melody (as most of the others from now on) exceeds a five-finger position, you must draw on your new knowledge of fingering devices when deciding on a fingering—then be sure to mark it in.

Somewhat similar to a round, because of its imitation, is a **canon.** Play this canon first as a duet—each player playing a single voice—then as a two-hand solo. (Here, again, you must work out fingering as the piece exceeds the five-finger position.)

## TALLIS' CANON

Thomas Tallis
Circa 1505–1585

*London Bridge* is so familiar that you can play it by ear. First sing the song and decide which degree of the five-finger position it begins on or if it exceeds the five-finger position. When you select a key in which to play, choose one which will bring the song well within the range of your singing voice. By writing the song down you will be able to mark in your choice of fingering, and accompanying chords. Indicate the chords by writing a I or $V_7$ under the appropriate melody-tone. (This is an elementary form of **figured bass**.)

By now the I $V_7$ I pattern is familiar to you. Warmup IV will help speed it up. Play it through all keys as rapidly as possible, being careful to strike the three tones of each chord exactly together.

### WARMUP IV

## Framing Chords from Above

In the last chapter you learned to frame chords at the keyboard. Now see if you can frame them *in the air*. With your right hand held high over the keyboard, assume the position which you think will exactly conform to a major triad, then bring your hand down slowly without the least change and see how nearly it fits the chord you are aiming for. Do this over a number of triads and keep score of your successes and failures.

Your skill in framing chords will help you in the next warmup, which consists of nothing but C major triads starting with the lowest on the keyboard and progressing up through each octave to the highest, then down again, alternating hands. When you can play the warmup as written, play it on all other major triads. In some keys you will find that you are an octave short so must play the last chord with your right hand instead of your left hand. Can you tell which keys these will be?

WARMUP V

## First Use of the Damper Pedal

As soon as you can play Warmup V perfectly in every key, you may use the pedal. As you strike the first chord, depress the right pedal (the **damper pedal**) with your right foot and hold it down for the duration of the warmup. If you make the slightest mistake, you must release the pedal immediately.

## The Subdominant Triad

Our new chord is the **subdominant triad,** or **IV chord,** indicated by IV. As with the V₇ chord, we will use it by rote for the present. It is approached from a major triad thus: the lowest voice is retained, the middle voice moves up one half step, the highest voice moves up one whole step.

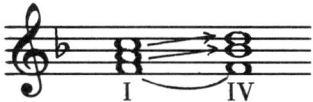

*Figure* 26.

Play I IV I in the keys of G, D, F, B, C♯, and A major.

This new chord will add a great deal to your harmonic resources, as you will discover when you harmonize the next songs. Play them in all keys, with the melody in either hand.

ROUSSEAU'S LULLABY

Attributed
Jean Jacques Rousseau
1712–1778

LAVENDER'S BLUE

English Folksong

## OH, SUSANNAH!

Stephen C. Foster
1826-1864

## Legato and Staccato

Until now you have been playing in as smooth and connected a manner as possible, releasing each key as you strike the next so that there is neither break between tones nor overlapping. You have been playing **legato.** All piano music is assumed to be legato unless otherwise indicated.

*In Lyric Piece No. II* we find such an indication. The dots over the accompaniment chords mean that the chords are to be played **staccato.** Theoretically, staccato marks halve the value of notes so that a quarter note with a dot over it would be equivalent to an eighth note followed by an eighth rest. In practice, however, the staccato mark is more an indication of touch than of tone duration. There are several kinds of staccato touch though all produce a short, detached sound. In *Lyric Piece No. II* the chords should be played with a slightly stroking motion, and the two chords in each measure should be exactly alike. As a preliminary exercise it would be helpful to play Warmup IV with staccato quarter notes.

The left hand in the first part of *Lyric Piece No. II* and the right hand in the second part would be played legato even without the slurs. The function of the slurs is to indicate phrasing. At the end of each phrase lift your hand a little. This is somewhat like breathing for a singer; it helps punctuate the music and makes it more intelligible. Experiment with dynamics and write them in.

# LYRIC PIECE NO. II

H. Hollins Banber

With the *Italian Hymn* we have our first formal duet. Here, two players share one keyboard—the upper player performing the *primo* (I°) part, the lower player performing the *secondo* (II$^{do}$) part. The players will not feel too crowded if the Primo pianist holds his left wrist rather high and plays toward the back of the keyboard, while the Secondo pianist drops his right wrist and plays toward the front of the keyboard. Before playing, decide on the tempo; then let one player establish the beat by counting a preliminary measure. The dotted lines leading from the right hand part to the left hand part in measures 7 and 8 show that in spite of a change in staff and hand, the melodic line is unbroken.

## ITALIAN HYMN
A Duet for Four Hands

E. de Giardini 1716–1796
Arranged by M. S. McLain

## Hand Gymnastics

Your new exercise, designed to strengthen fingers, is of the variety known as *isometric*, which means *pushing against yourself* — and that is exactly what you do.

CHAPTER THREE

In turn, push your thumb against the tip of your second finger, then against the tip of your third finger, then fourth and fifth. Count four in a moderate tempo, pressing together on the count of "one" and relaxing on the count of "four." Do this four or five times for each finger. The trick is not to let the first joint of any finger collapse or buckle. Try to make a circle with the thumb and each finger.

## Rhythm Drill

## Sight-Reading

Memory plays an important part in sight-reading. Once you have identified a given chord, you should not have to reexamine each of its elements when the chord is repeated, but simply recognize the collection of notes as a *single symbol* of a now-familiar chord. This is known as **cluster,** or **note-group,** reading, and is analogous to the simultaneous perception of several words, or even sentences, by a rapid reader of books. Only a very defective reader spells out each word letter by letter.

For musicians such as singers and performers on orchestral instruments, reading *two* staves at once often presents difficulties—the player being torn between trying to focus his eyes first on the upper staff, then on the lower. Consider, though, how you perceive a house or a picture or a landscape. If a house, you note at once its style, color, and materials; whether the door is in front or at the side; how many stories it has; if the windows have awnings; what flowers, shrubs, trees—if any—adorn it, and so on. If a picture, you can observe in an instant the table with its green covering and bowl of fruit; the carved Victorian chair with the sleeping cat; the open window whose fluttering curtain affords a glimpse of blue sky and fleecy clouds. And how long does it take to discern in a landscape the broad meadow with its solitary elm beneath which stand two white horses, as though to take shelter from menacing storm-clouds above?

If you can absorb all these details at a glance, it will be no great task for you to note the symbols on two staves in a space scarcely an inch-and-a-half square! Just relax your gaze, letting your glance move easily *between* the staves and seeing the ten bracketed lines as a *single* picture.

While you should not "try over" ahead of time the material to be sight-read, it is always advisable to survey it silently and briefly, checking on accidentals, rhythms, unfamiliar notes, ledger lines, clef and possible change of clef, and of course key signatures and time signatures. Sometimes an unexpected density of rests and notes will cause a player to panic and fumble a passage which is in reality quite simple. For example, in No. 1 below, the second half looks "fussier" than the first half, but is really the same: the left-hand chord is merely delayed for one count, then struck twice. Likewise, in No. 3 the single bass notes in the second half are simply notes of the chords which appeared in the first half. A preliminary survey of these studies would make such matters clear before the player confronted them in actual performance.

In the following sight-reading studies you will need the assistance of your piano-mate in operating the pacer since you will be using both hands at the keyboard. You should be able to read one full measure ahead if you have made a proper preliminary examination.

## Improvisation

You may now combine the $V_7$ chord with the I chord in your improvisations, but confine your melody to those tones which are to be found in the two chords, using the tones of the I chord when the tonic harmony prevails and the tones of the $V_7$ chord when that harmony prevails. Improvise in all keys, with the melody sometimes in the right hand and sometimes in the left. Make use of different meters: $\frac{2}{4} \frac{3}{4} \frac{4}{4} \frac{6}{8}$. The models (Figures 27 and 28) will suggest other ways in which to combine your materials.

*Figure 27.*

*Figure* 28.

It may occur to you that there are two ways in which to approach your subject: if you are thinking melodically, you have only to accompany the melody, but if this is difficult, you may plot out a chord progression and construct a melody from the available tones. It is not easy to restrict yourself to chord-tones in developing a melody, but by limiting your resources you will gain skill in handling them.

There is still another way to "get off the ground" and that is to use an already established beginning as a springboard and take off from there. The first two measures of Figures 27 and 28 could serve this purpose. Figures 29 and 30 provide two more starts. Add four more measures to Figure 29 to make eight measures in all, and add two measures to Figure 30 to make four measures in all. Be sure that you end on the tonic harmony.

*Figure* 29.

*Figure* 30.

## ⋆ Hearsay and Other Ear Work

1. Identify isolated chords as I, IV, or $V_7$ chords.
2. After the key is given, repeat at one piano what the teacher or another student plays at a second piano (I, IV, and $V_7$ chords).
3. Repeat, by clapping or tapping, a simple rhythm dictated by the teacher. These should be no more complicated than those suggested in Figure 31.

*Figure* 31.

4. Play and harmonize *This Old Man* by ear, in all keys.

## ⋆ Review and Suggested Assignments

1. Define the following terms or symbols:
   round; canon; *f; cresc.; primo; secondo;* figured bass; keyboard feel; note group; legato; staccato; phrase; dynamics; *D.C. al Fine;* voice; part.
2. Work out fingering for each of the melodies and give reasons for your choices.
3. Transpose *Frère Jacques* into all major keys, playing the melody with either hand and harmonizing with the other.
4. Work out a satisfactory fingering for *Tallis' Canon*, write it in your music and practice until you can play it smoothly and easily, hands together.

5. Work out a satisfactory fingering for both *primo* and *secondo* parts of the *Italian Hymn*, then learn to play each part smoothly.

6. Write out, finger, then harmonize *London Bridge*. Transpose it into all keys. Play the melody with each hand, harmonizing with the other. Do the same with *Twinkle, Twinkle, Little Star*.

7. After you have mastered Warmup V, play $V_7$ chords in the same way, then IV chords.

8. Create, write down, and perform your own rhythm drills.

# ✳ 4 ✳

## Minor Mode

### THEME FROM THE FOURTH SYMPHONY

Tchaik(
1840–

Although the key signature of this *Theme* has neither sharps nor flats, it is not the key of C major but of A minor, which is the **relative minor** of C major. Relative minor keys are found three half steps below major keys and have the same signature.

You will notice that the five-finger position here extends from A through E, but where is the half step? The position of the half step is what makes the difference between a major and a minor five-finger position. In major the half step occurs between the third and fourth degrees, while in minor it occurs between the second and third degrees.

MAJOR         MINOR

1 2 3̲ 4 5    1 2̲ 3 4 5

To convert this minor melody to a major melody, all you need do is *raise* the third degree a half step from C to C♯. This also works in reverse: you have only to *lower* the third degree of a major five-finger position or triad to make it minor.

Capital letters usually are used to indicate major keys; small letters (lower case) to indicate minor keys. In the reading matter of this text, however, capital letters followed by "major" or "minor" are used for easier identification.

Playing a five-finger position first, then a triad, change:

| C  | to | c  | b♭  | B♭ |
|----|----|----|-----|----|
| G  |    | g  | c♯  | C♯ |
| E  |    | e  | a   | A  |
| F♯ |    | f♯ | f   | F  |
| B  |    | b  | a♭  | A♭ |
| E♭ |    | e♭ | D   | d  |

### MINOR-MAJOR BOOGIE

M. S. McLain

*There are two methods of writing chromatic scales. The first is to combine the tones of the major and minor scales on any given tonic, raise the fourth degree and lower the second degree. The second method is to raise (sharp or natural) black keys or non-scale tones on the way up and lower (flat or natural) them on the way down.

To establish the minor-major element in this composition, the first method has been used in the left-hand part of the first measure. After that, however, the second method has been employed because three accidentals could thereby be eliminated, thus presenting a simpler picture to the eye.

The $V_7$ chord is exactly the same in minor as in major, but since its middle note is approached from a location a half step lower in minor than in major, the middle voice must move up a *whole step*, rather than a half step, to compensate.

*Figure* 32.

Warmup VI will make this clear. Play it through all major and minor keys, hands separately first, then hands together. When you can play the warmup fluently, play it with eyes closed or hands covered.

Roman capitals (I, V) are used for major triads; lower case Roman numerals (i, iv) are used for minor triads.

### WARMUP VI

Unlike the $V_7$ chord, which is the same in both major and minor, the subdominant triad follows the **mode** of the tonic and so will be slightly different in minor mode. In this case the lowest tone is retained, the third moves up a *whole step*, and the fifth moves up a *half step*.

*Figure* 33.

Play Warmup VII in accordance with directions for Warmup VI.

### WARMUP VII

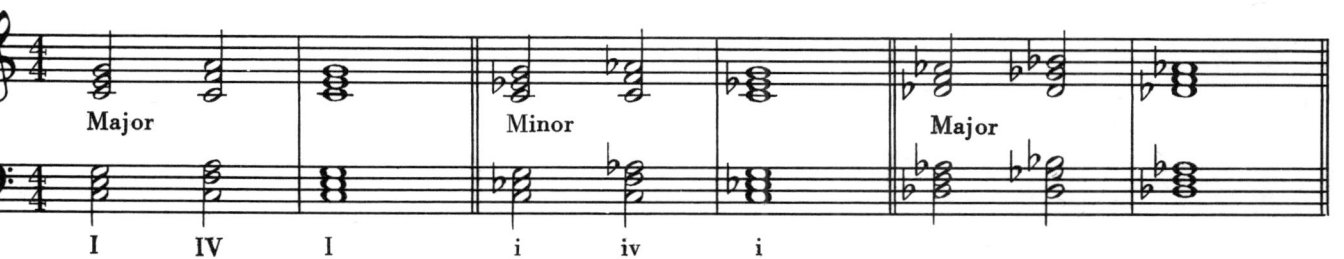

When you understand the I IV I and I $V_7$ I patterns in both major and minor, you may combine them into a I IV I $V_7$ I, i iv i $V_7$ i sequence and play it through all keys. This will be:

### WARMUP VIII

The next melody is in minor mode and the harmony is indicated. Play a chord on the first and second counts, allowing a quarter rest for the third count. (This type of accompaniment is more rhythmical and less monotonous than the plodding, one-chord-to-the-count variety.)

Play the melody with the left hand as well as with the right hand.

WAYFARING STRANGER

American Spiritual

This melody covers a more extensive range than the other melodies you have been playing, so, for the present, do not transpose it.

## Octaves

Next to the fifth, the most important interval for the pianist to feel is the **octave.** Slow octaves are usually played by lifting the forearm from the elbow and keeping the wrist immobile. Lift the hand two or three inches above the keyboard for each stroke and keep the octave framed as you did with the triads. Never permit your hand to collapse or deviate from the octave span.

*Figure* 34.

### WARMUP IX

Rapid octaves are played with a relaxed wrist stroke, always keeping the octaves framed. A pianist's wrists can become very tired if he is not used to playing octaves or lets himself grow tense. For this reason, he should use any notes of relatively longer duration—in this case the quarter notes—as resting points, while still keeping the octave framed.

Play Warmup X chromatically up and down one octave. Do not continue after your wrist becomes tired, but rest one hand while playing with the other. Your endurance will increase gradually.

### WARMUP X

# WARMUP XI

## Names of Octaves

The octaves on the keyboard and Grand Staff are designated as follows:

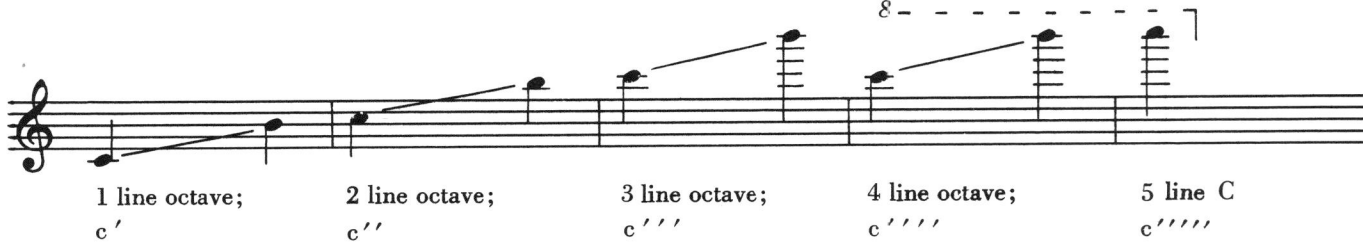

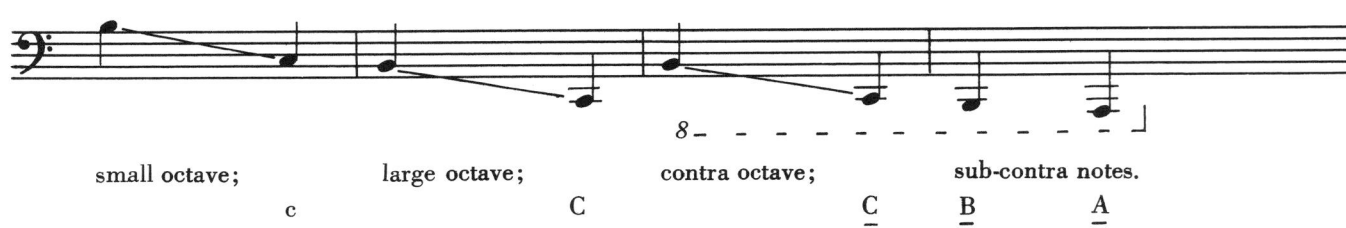

*Figure* 35.

Listen carefully as you play chords and single-note sequences in each octave so that you will be able to recognize the location of music you hear.

## Hand Gymnastics

These exercises will help your wrist to be more flexible in octave playing. You may do them at the keyboard, on a table's edge, or on any surface which is approximately on a level with your elbow.

A. Assume an octave span on the real or imaginary keys, then—always keeping your thumb and fifth finger firmly in place—drop your wrist as far down as it will go and raise it as high as it will go. Do this eight times.

B. Again assume the octave span, your wrist on a level with the back of your hand. This time keep your *forearm* in an unchanged position, but throw your hand back as far as it will go—still framed to the octave span. Do this in a moderate tempo eight times.

## Harmonizing Warmups

In Chapter 2 you were asked to harmonize Warmup II with the I and $V_7$ chords. You can now harmonize Warmups IX and XI with I, IV, and $V_7$. Study how best to place these chords. You can play the new arrangements as solos or as duets. Try them both ways and in all major and minor keys.

Play Warmups II, III, and V in minor mode, and harmonize Warmup II.

CRUSADERS' TUNE
(A Duet for Four Hands)

St. Anthony's Chorale
Arranged by M. S. McLain

48  CLASS PIANO

# CHORALE
from *The Passion According to St. Matthew*
(A Duet for Four Hands)

J. S. Bach
1685–1750

## SONG OF THE VOLGA BOATMEN

Traditional Russian Song
Arranged by M. S. McLa...

## Sight-Reading

Many people are less familiar with the notes of the bass staff than with those of the treble staff. The next three exercises should help you find your way with greater ease.

The next exercises should be played with *covered hands*. It is quite useless to say firmly that you will not look and therefore need not cover your hands; before you know what is happening your eyes will sneak a peek. Avoid this wear and tear on your willpower and cover your hands. The best way to do this is with a newspaper opened full width, then folded top to bottom. The paper can be anchored behind the keyboard cover or secured on the music rack by a book or two. In any case, let the paper hang down over your hands and don't peek underneath. Get your bearings by feeling the groups of two and three black keys. The newspaper, folded properly, will cover more than four octaves.

## Four Solos

These pieces are designed to help you gain keyboard feel, and you should learn to play them without looking at your hands.

In *Pentatonia*, only black keys are used. If you place the fingers of both hands over the keys which are to be played you will not have to look at your hands again.

The feel of the octave span in the left hand is an important feature of *Club Zara*. To maintain contact with this interval, give up the usual five-finger position and play the first note of the piece with the third finger. In the tenth measure, pass the 2nd finger of your left hand over the thumb for one note. In the ninth measure the interval, B♮ to A♭, between the fourth and third fingers of your right hand, may feel awkward, but later, when you have scales with standard fingering, you will encounter this same interval (an **augmented second**) in the **harmonic** form of the minor scale, and it will help if you are already familiar with the feel of it. The same interval occurs in the left hand two measures later. Needless to say, this should be practiced hands separately before being played hands together.

In the *Old French Carol*, the right hand employs a number of the fingering devices you have learned. The left hand, however, is framed to a triad throughout the entire piece, only changing to adjust to the slight modifications of shape caused by black keys. It moves away from, then back to, the initial chord—first a whole tone, then two whole tones, and so on, each move covering a greater distance. You must learn to calculate these hand shifts by feel rather than by looking. This will not be difficult if you analyze what is involved in each shift and practice it separately:

*First shift:* G minor triad to F minor triad. Hand holds same position, outside fingers moving to nearest white neighbor below, middle finger finding nearest black neighbor below. Reverse procedure for return.

*Second shift:* G minor to E♭ major. This is easy because in the G minor triad you already have two tones of the E♭ major triad. Just before you are ready to make the shift, lift your third and first fingers (still holding your fifth finger down) and place them over the G and B♭. (Your little finger, still on G, is your guide.) Then move the little finger—by feel—down to E♭ and strike the chord. On the way back, reverse the process, bringing the fifth finger up to G, then sliding 3 and 1 to B♭ and D.

*Third shift:* G minor to D minor. When you are ready to shift, move your thumb down to touch (but not strike) A. You can test this by touching your little finger with your thumb, then locating the neighboring white key above. With your thumb on A, move 5 and 3 down to frame a white-key triad on D. On the return, bring your little finger up to the key just below your thumb to locate G, and shift 3 and 1 up to frame the G minor triad. Another way to reach the D minor triad from a G minor triad is to move your little finger down to D, identifying it by the feel of the octave span between it and the thumb, which is still on the higher D. With 5 on the lower D, move 3 and 1 down to F and A, which you will identify by the feel of the triad. On the return, your thumb will reach up to establish the octave span from D to D, and 5 and 3 will move up to frame the triad.

*Fourth shift:* G minor to C minor. Move your thumb to G, already occupied by the fifth finger, and shift 5 and 3 to C and E♭. Remember to feel for a black key with your third finger. To return, put your fifth finger on G in place of your thumb and frame the G minor triad with 3 and 1.

The first phrase of the *Maypole Dance* keeps the right hand in one five-finger position, so you can give most of your attention to the left hand. The left-hand thumb acts as "anchor man" and repeats the same note, but the fifth finger, after starting on the tonic, reaches out to explore two new keys at increasing distances from the thumb, then returns. These new keys — A♯ and G♯ —, being black, are easy to locate. In the next two measures the fifth finger stays "on location" but the thumb goes exploring. Here again, the black keys help it to find its way. In the second phrase the right hand maintains a five-finger position for a measure and a half, then shifts to another five-finger position. An octave span returns it to the first five-finger position. The right-hand part can claim most of your attention because the left hand is merely seesawing back and forth on one octave span.

All of this is cumbersome to explain but quite easy to do. You will be surprised at how quickly and securely you will be able to find your way over the keyboard without looking. You will begin to reap "tangible" dividends from the effort you invested in learning to frame triads and octaves.

PENTATONIA

M. S. McLai

## CLUB ZARA

M. S. McLain

## OLD FRENCH CAROL

Arranged by
M. S. McLain

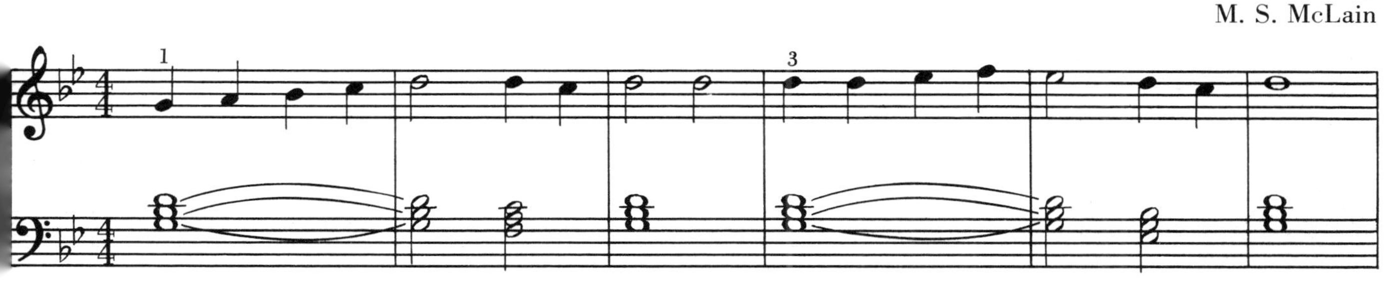

CHAPTER FOUR

## MAYPOLE DANCE

M. S. McLain

## Rhythm Drill

This rhythm drill combines tapping with pedal action. Use the damper pedal. Always keep your right foot in contact with it, even when it is not depressed. Do not allow any sounds of the mechanism to be heard. The lines under the notes are one way of indicating pedal action. Go through the drills tapping with your right hand, then do them again tapping with your left hand.

## Improvisation

Your new vocabulary will include the IV chord. Although you will still restrict your melodies to chord tones, you may include two tonics, an octave apart, and you may use minor mode.

The directions in Chapter 3 regarding meters and keys apply equally to work in this chapter.

Figures 36 and 37 will suggest many other possibilities to you.

*Figure 36.*

*Figure 37.*

## ★ Hearsay and Other Ear Work

1. Clap or tap rhythms or metric combinations of two to four measures which your teacher dictates to you.
2. Dictate, by clapping or tapping, rhythms or metric combinations of two to four measures, to your classmates.
3. Play, after your teacher (piano-to-piano dictation), short melodic phrases. You may hear each phrase twice, and if you wish, you may sing or hum the phrase before playing it. The important thing is not to try out different notes on the keyboard until you stumble on the right ones, but to identify the correct tones before you begin to play.
4. Identify I, i, IV, iv, and $V_7$ chords as your teacher plays them.
5. Identify the octave location of chords and melodic phrases played by other students or your teacher.
6. Strike a key in your vocal range and, taking it as the lowest tone in a triad, sing the two higher tones of the triad. Strike another tone in another key and, considering it the middle voice in a triad, sing the lowest and highest tones. Again, strike a new note which will be the highest tone of a triad,

---

*The B (2nd degree of the five-finger position), although omitted in this form of the $V_7$ chord, is a true part of the chord and so may be used in the melody.

and sing the two lower tones. Do this in a number of keys, both major and minor.

7. In this exercise, choose a tone in your vocal range and consider it successively the lowest, middle, then highest voice in a major, then a minor, triad. Play this constant pitch but *sing* the other tones which make up the six triads.

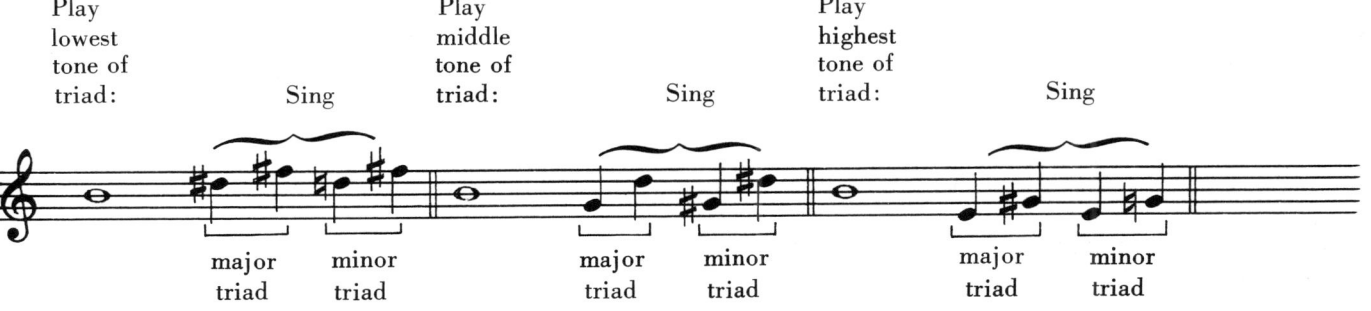

*Figure* 38.

8. Play and harmonize *For He's a Jolly Good Fellow* and *Pop Goes the Weasel* by ear in all keys.

### ★ Review and Suggested Assignments

1. Define the following terms or symbols:
   mode; 1-line g; 2-line g; 3-line g; f´; f´´; f´´´; brace; e; B; C̲; A̲; *p*; *mp*; *mf*; *f*; pentatonic; *espressivo*; stepwise; chordwise; figure.
2. By their shapes, identify the following "pictures" as I, IV, or V₇ chords:

*Figure* 39.

3. Change numbers 1 and 3 of the sight-reading studies in Chapter 3 from major to minor.
4. Play *Lyric Piece No. II* with covered hands.
5. Sight-read the bass clef exercises until you can recognize each note readily. Then turn the page upside down and recite the names of the notes as they now appear.
6. Learn the *Four Solos* and play them with your hands covered.
7. Play the left-hand part of *Minor-Major Boogie* in all keys.

# ✶ 5 ✶

## Major Scales in Tetrachords

When you play a IV chord you extend the five-finger position upward by one scale degree. When you play a $V_7$ chord you extend the five-finger position downward one scale degree. These two additional notes in combination with the notes of the five-finger position give all the degrees of a major scale—the IV chord providing the sixth degree, the $V_7$ providing the seventh. By putting the seventh degree up an octave so that it follows the sixth, and repeating the first degree, or tonic, an octave higher, we have a complete scale from 1 to 8. This also applies to minor scales but we will consider them later.

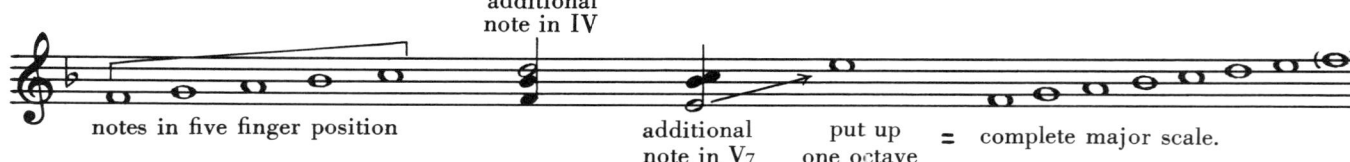

*Figure* 40.

Dividing these eight tones into four lower and four higher tones gives us two **tetrachords,** which are not chords in the usual sense at all, but a diatonic series of four notes each. If you examine these tetrachords you will observe that they are structurally alike: whole steps between each of the lower three tones, but only a half step between the third and fourth tones. In other words, the half steps in a major scale occur between the third and fourth, and between the seventh and eighth degrees.

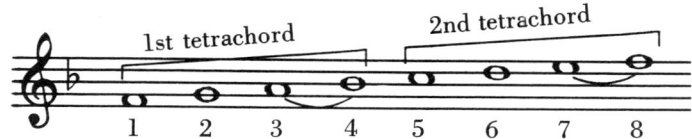

*Figure* 41.

For a while we will play our scales in tetrachords—the lower tetrachord with the left hand, the upper tetrachord with the right hand. There are several reasons for doing this. One is that the fingering is the same for all scales, thus eliminating fingering problems. Another is that by having a different finger for every key you can *see* the entire scale spread out like a map under your hands before you begin to play. You will not use your thumbs, so fold them under and close to the palms of each hand and *keep them there* while you play.

*Figure* 42.

When you are able to organize and play easily the eight tones of every major scale, try extending the scales over two octaves. To do this, simply strike the highest tonic of the first octave once with the fifth finger of the right hand, then again with the fifth finger of the left hand, and continue up the second octave, thus:

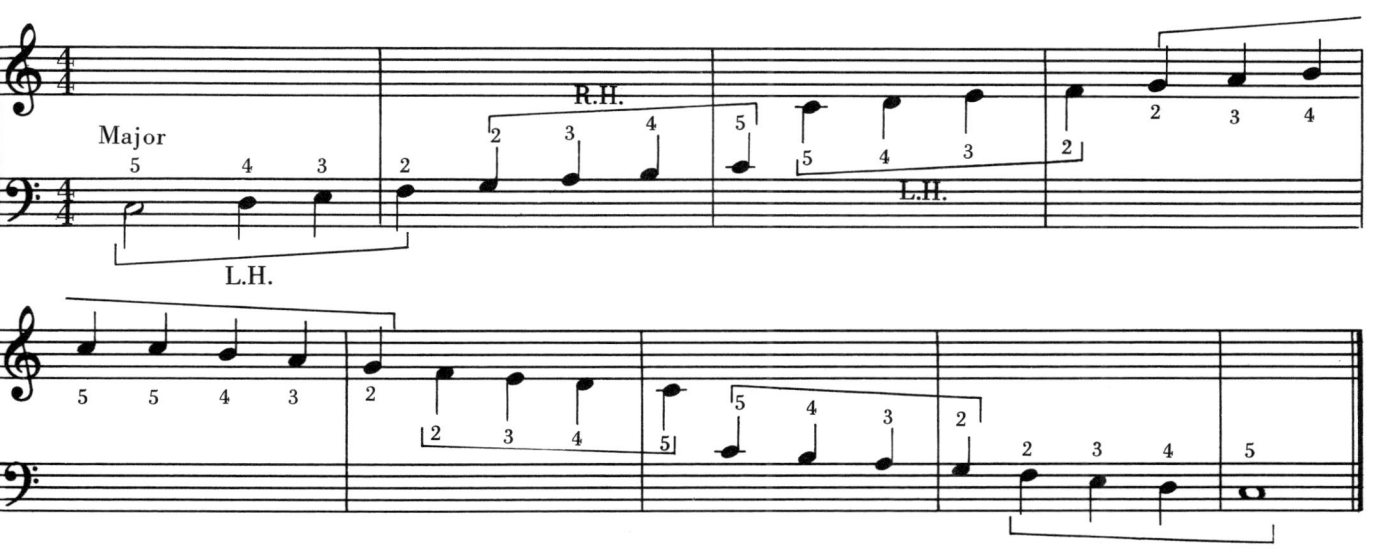

*Figure* 43.

## Scale-Degree Names

You have already learned that the first degree of any scale is called the tonic. Let us now consider the names of the other scale degrees. They are easy to remember because they are descriptive. After the tonic, the most important scale degree (for acoustical, theoretical, and philosophical reasons which we need not explore here) is the fifth—the **dominant**—hence its name. If we descend five degrees from the tonic, we arrive at the fourth degree of the scale, and since it is five degrees *under* the tonic it is called the **subdominant.** Halfway between the tonic and the dominant is the third—the **mediant** (note the similar words with similar meanings: medium, median, mediate), and halfway between the tonic and subdominant is an underneath third—the sixth degree of the scale—which is called the **submediant.** This leaves only two scale degrees unnamed: the second and seventh. The second is called the **supertonic,** which is self-explanatory; the seventh is called the **leading tone** because of its strong tendency to move or "lead" to the tonic. There is one circumstance in which the seventh is not called the leading tone and this is when, as in the **pure,** or **natural,** form of the minor (see Chapter 6), the seventh degree is a *whole* step below the tonic instead of a half step. In this case it is called the **subtonic.** This distinction is frequently ignored, however, and more often than not you will hear the seventh degrees of all scales referred to as leading tones.

In order, they are:

| Scale degree | Name |
| --- | --- |
| 1st | TONIC |
| 2nd | SUPERTONIC |
| 3rd | MEDIANT |
| 4th | SUBDOMINANT |
| 5th | DOMINANT |
| 6th | SUBMEDIANT |
| 7th | LEADING TONE (or SUBTONIC) |
| 8th | TONIC |

*The First Noel* is a two-hand melody which incorporates an ascending major scale. Say the scale-degree *numbers* as you play it, and transpose it into every major key.

## THE FIRST NOEL

Traditional English Carol

Another song which incorporates a major scale is *Joy to the World*. Play this by ear in several keys. Start on black keys as well as white keys, and of course, play it tetrachord-wise.

## Change-Ringing—and Playing

The twelve-tone "row" concept, or numerically planned sequences of pitches, is not new; it has been the practice of bell-ringers, particularly in England, for hundreds of years. The permutations, or sequential combinations of which any given number of bells is capable, are called **changes.** It has been estimated that twelve bells could produce 479,001,600 changes which would take 37 years and 355 days to ring.

Without embarking on any such formidable venture, we can still enjoy a taste of change-ringing by playing some of the changes on the keyboard, and what better way *really* to learn scales?

Place your fingers, tetrachord-fashion, over the C-major scale. The first four changes, in music notation, are shown in Figure 44. After you have played all the changes in C major, play them in other major keys. Say, or sing, the scale-degree numbers as you play.

*Figure* 44.

CHAPTER FIVE 63

## HUNTING UP AND COURSING DOWN

```
8 7 6 5 4 3 2 1
7 8 5 6 3 4 2 1
7 5 8 3 6 2 4 1
5 7 3 8 2 6 4 1
5 3 7 2 8 4 6 1
3 5 2 7 4 8 6 1
3 2 5 4 7 6 8 1
2 3 4 5 6 7 8 1
2 4 3 6 5 8 7 1
4 2 6 3 8 5 7 1
4 6 2 8 3 7 5 1
6 4 8 2 7 3 5 1
6 8 4 7 2 5 3 1
8 6 7 4 5 2 3 1
8 7 6 5 4 3 2 1
```

The title "Hunting Up and Coursing Down" refers to the way in which the "lead" or highest bell moves one position further away from first place in each change. This is "hunting up." "Coursing down" is the return journey to first place.

## The Circle of Keys

If you look back over the first eight warmups, you will notice that they all begin with either a five-finger position or a triad. In both cases the lowest note was the tonic and the highest note the dominant. You have played these warmups in what we called **chromatic order,** that is, ascending or descending a half step for each repetition. Now let us try them in a new way. Taking the highest tone of the five-finger position or triad (the dominant) as the new tonic of a new key, Warmup I would progress like this:

*Figure* 45.

This is called **playing in dominant order,** and if you continue through enough keys in this way you eventually will return to the key from which you started. You may also do this in **subdominant order.** Progressing through all the keys in this manner is known as **making the circle**—or **cycle—of fifths;** or, if in subdominant order, **making the circle of fourths.** When you examine Figure 46 you will observe that as you move to the right, or clockwise, from C, each new key will have an additional sharp or one less flat. As you move to the left from C, each key will have an additional flat or one less sharp. The three pairs of bracketed keys represent a continuation of the same pattern—the sharp keys moving clockwise around to C♯, which has seven sharps, and the flat keys moving counterclockwise around to C♭, which has seven flats. It so happens that for each of these pairs the pitch is the same (on the piano) although the "spelling" is different. To such a relationship we give the term **enharmonic.**

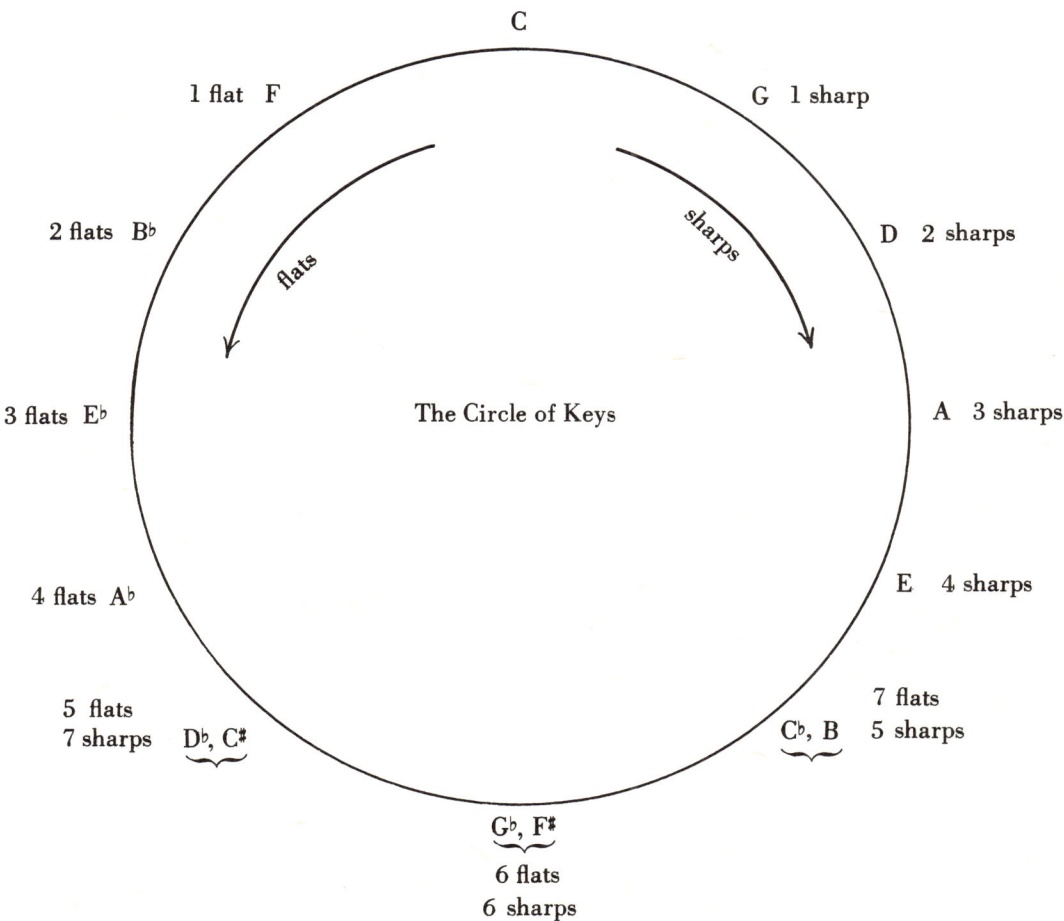

*Figure* 46.

Play all the warmups in dominant order, then in subdominant order. Warmup XII is given here in dominant order, but can be played as well in subdominant order or up or down chromatically.

WARMUP XII

## Harmonizing Each Degree of the Scale

Now that our melodies are covering a wider range, let us consider how each scale degree in the octave may be harmonized, using those chords of which the melody tone is part.

| MELODY TONE | | CHORD |
|---|---|---|
| 1 | may be harmonized with | I and IV |
| 2 | | $V_7$ |
| 3 | | I |
| 4 | | IV and $V_7$ |
| 5 | | I and $V_7$ |
| 6 | | IV |
| 7 | | $V_7$ |

*Figure* 47.

## Three Melodies to Harmonize and Transpose

**Fingering.** The increased range of the melodies and songs will mean hand shifts and fingering adjustments. Since fingerings differ in different keys, only general provisions can be made. For instance, always begin with a finger which will allow you to make maximum use of all your other fingers. Don't start a downward passage in the left hand with your fifth finger. If you find yourself in danger of running out of fingers don't wait until the emergency is upon you: put two or three fingers over or pass your thumb under (depending on direction), or use a contraction which, when "let out," will give you a greater reach.

**Transposition.** To transpose the new songs, follow these steps which are basically the same as those you have been following.

1. Play melody alone in original key, singing scale-degree numbers.
2. Determine which scale degree the melody begins on.
3. Choose new key.
4. Play tetrachord scale up and down one octave in new key, saying scale-degree numbers aloud, and *paying particular attention to the location of* 6 *and* 7. (Remember, it is easier to find 7 by counting *down* one half step from 8 than by counting *up* seven degrees from 1.)
5. Locate first note. (Same *scale degree* in new key as it was in original key.)
6. Play melody with one hand alone.
7. Harmonize melody.

THEME FROM THE "*NEW WORLD*" *SYMPHONY*

Antonin Dvořák
1841–1904

CHAPTER FIVE 67

## OLD BLACK JOE

Stephen C. Foster

## SWANEE RIVER

Stephen C. Foster

# Rhythm Drill

## Non-Harmonic Tones

In the chord guide (Figure 47) only those chords which *included* the melody tone were given. The same principle in reverse has governed your improvisation: you have been limited to using only chord tones in your melodies.

Many beautiful melodies found in music literature are fashioned from these tones alone, but such a practice is necessarily restrictive. If you look back over the melodies and songs which you have been harmonizing, you will find that in general only chord tones were accompanied by a chord, on strong beats. However, many non-chord tones occurred *between* the chord tones, giving the music a flowing character as well as greater variety and interest. These non-chord tones are called **non-harmonic tones.**

**A non-harmonic tone is any tone which is not part of the immediate harmony.**

Theorists have organized these non-harmonic tones into many categories depending on their function, the direction in which they move, how they are approached and left, whether they fall on accented beats or unaccented beats, and whether they remain in or move out of the diatonic pattern.

Among the classifications are (in alphabetical order) accented passing tones; accented upper neighbors; anticipations; appoggiaturas; changing tones; chromatic lower neighbors; échappées; embellishments; escape tones; inverted suspensions; neighboring tones; passing tones; pedals; retardations.

Before despair overtakes you, let it be said that some of these terms have the same meaning, and not all of them are used by any one theorist. Indeed, theorists are by no means in agreement as to terminology and usage. Moreover, these are matters which more appropriately belong in the harmony or counterpoint class than in the piano class, so, for our very practical purpose, let us reduce these confusing categories to their basic and common elements.

1. All non-harmonic tones are dissonant because they never belong to the prevailing harmony.

2. Most non-harmonic tones pass from one chord tone to another and so are called **passing tones.** Some passing tones occur on weak beats or weak parts of beats, as part of a free-flowing melody (**unaccented passing tones**), in which case the dissonance is scarcely discernible. Others occur on strong beats (**accented passing tones**), where their dissonant quality is more pronounced.

3. All non-harmonic tones ultimately move (resolve) to a chord tone in the same voice.

4. In general, non-harmonic tones are drawn from the degrees of the diatonic scale, but the note one half-step below a scale tone, approached from and returning to that scale tone, is used frequently. When this non-harmonic tone happens not to belong to the scale, a *chromatic alteration* is involved (**chromatic lower neighbors**).

We should bear in mind that ideas of beauty and logic in music give rise to the rules—not the reverse. Over the years our ears as well as our concepts of beauty and logic have undergone many modifications. What was once considered offensive is now not only acceptable but charming, and may even have become trite. The rules are constantly being relaxed and changed. As scholars you should be familiar with the names and habits of the non-harmonic tones, but as "functional" musicians (and especially as improvisers, required to execute a complex maneuver in a limited time-span) your purpose will be better served by listening to the finest music so that you may develop your taste, and then acquiring skill in playing what your inner ear and good taste dictate.

Before going on to the new pieces, reexamine all the songs and melodies you have harmonized up to this point and identify accented and unaccented non-harmonic tones.

Three of the pieces which follow contain accented passing tones. Those in the *Menuet in F Major* by W. A. Mozart are harsh because they fall on the strongest beat in the measure and are held for an appreciable time. Those in the Bach *Menuet* and Haydn *German Dance* in D Major are barely noticeable because, though falling on the strong part of the beat, they move quickly along and sometimes are unaccompanied. Listen to their effect—obvious or subtle—in the otherwise bland course of the music. They are marked * and will serve as models when you encounter similar examples in the songs which you will be harmonizing.

MINUET IN A MINOR

Henry Purcell
1658(?)–1695

# MENUET IN F MAJOR

Wolfgang Amadeus Mozart
1757–1791

# GERMAN DANCE IN D MAJOR

Joseph Haydn
1732–1809

MINUET IN G MAJOR, NO. I

J. S. Bach

†See section on embellishments in Chapter 10 for this and future embellishments.

CHAPTER FIVE 73

## CIRCLE GAME

M. S. McLai

Here are two new songs to harmonize and transpose. Each has an accented non-harmonic tone where the harmony is indicated.

WINTER, GOOD-BYE

Folk Song

OLD SONG

Traditional

## Sight-Reading

Since ledger lines sometimes are bothersome in sight-reading, a few hints may help you cope with them.

1. Frequently a note perched high (or low) on a ledger line is an octave away from the preceding note on the staff. This is the case in the initial part of each of the first two exercises. Do not attempt to count lines and spaces, but learn to recognize the *spatial* distance between the two notes, remembering always that an octave is a line-and-space, or even-numbered, interval. Regardless of staff degrees,

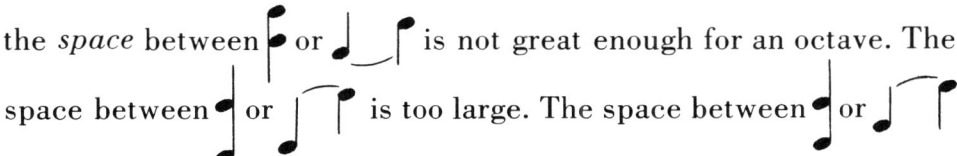

is right and you should recognize it as an octave, even though you do not know which octave. The distance between the lines of the staff and the ledger lines varies according to the kind of type used by the printer, but your eye should easily relate the octave "picture" to the dimensions, or gauge, of the staff from which you are reading.

2. When you do not have a lower note to guide you, you must establish fixed points from which to get your bearings. The best ones are the second ledger line above the treble staff and the second ledger line below the bass staff. Each is a C and from these you can make lightning calculations, knowing that every additional ledger line means an additional third, and also knowing that intervals on two lines *or* two spaces will be odd-numbered intervals, while those on lines *and* spaces will be even-numbered intervals. This may seem complicated at first, but it is infinitely quicker than laboriously counting up each line and space individually.

With practice, other ledger lines will become as familiar to you as the lines of the staff. You can hardly have a close acquaintance with  and not be aware that  is A, and almost as soon know that  is the picture of E.

1. 

2.

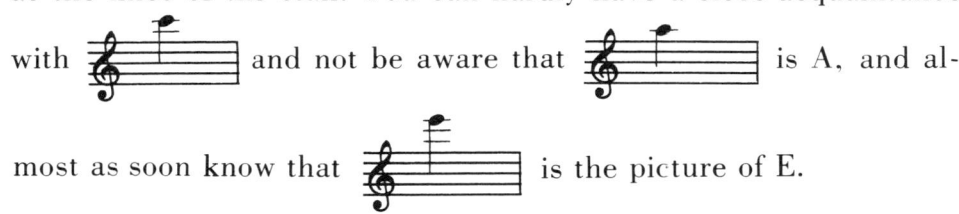

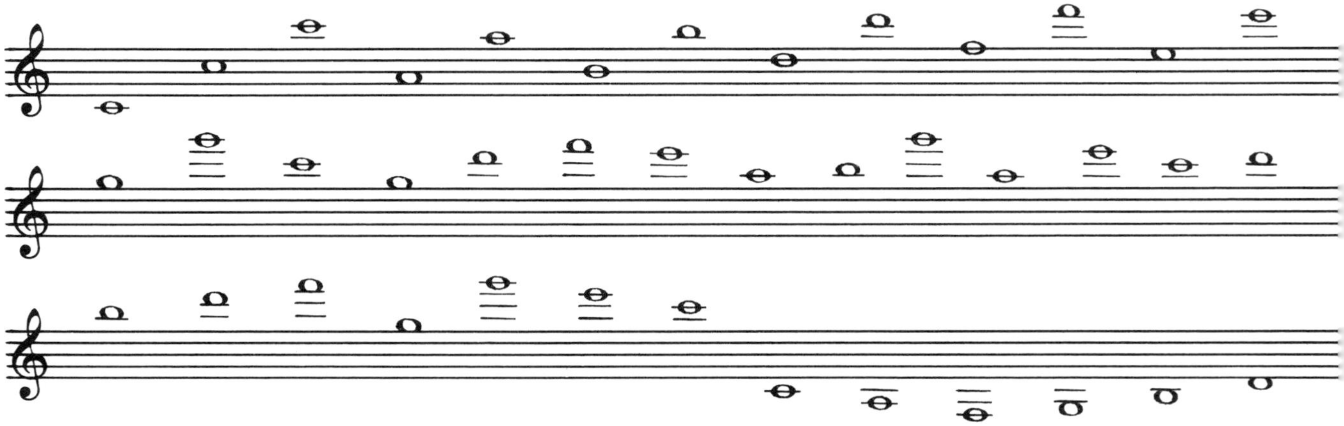

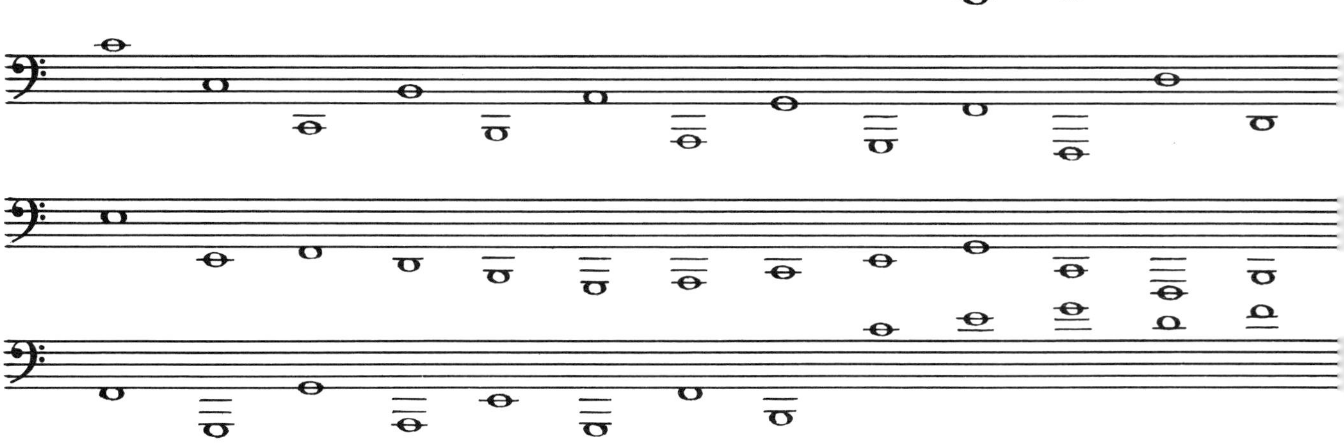

Play the next exercise with covered hands, and looking one measure ahead.

## Improvisation

You may now introduce passing tones in your improvisation, but stay with the unaccented variety for the present. Develop each of the beginnings (Figures 48, 49, 50) into two four-measure phrases (eight measures in all). Each beginning could be continued in a number of different ways. How many can you invent?

*Figure* 48.

CHAPTER FIVE 77

*Figure* 49.

*Figure* 50.

### ✶ Hearsay and Other Ear Work

1. Listen carefully as someone plays a scale slowly up and down one octave. Now identify the various scale degrees when they are *not* played in order but at random.
2. As the teacher or a student plays a familiar tune and stops at various points in its course, try to identify the scale degree on which the tune broke off.
3. Play *Joy to the World* and *Three Blind Mice* by ear and tetrachord-wise in all major keys. You may also play the latter as a round.
4. Play and harmonize *Yankee Doodle*, *Silent Night*, and *Auld Lang Syne* by ear, and in all keys.

### ✶ Review and Suggested Assignments

1. Define the following terms:
    tetrachord; chromatic order; dominant order; subdominant order; circle of fifths; circle of fourths; enharmonic; leading tone; mediant; supertonic; submediant; subtonic; ledger line; leger line; non-harmonic tone; passing tone; accented passing tone; unaccented passing tone.
2. Explain the names of the scale degrees.
3. On a staff of this gauge, which pairs of notes would form octaves?

*Figure* 51.

4. Study the ledger-line sight-reading exercises until all the notes are familiar to you, then turn the page upside down and read the names of the notes as they now appear. (Supply an imaginary bass clef for the notes below the staff and an imaginary treble clef for the notes above the staff.)

5. Place your hands over the two tetrachords of any scale and play individual scale degrees which someone else dictates, such as 6, 1, 5, 7, 2, 8, 3, 7, 4, and so on. Do this as rapidly as possible and in a number of keys.

6. Again play scale degrees as rapidly as possible from dictation, but do not place your hands over tetrachords; instead, play every note with the second finger of your right hand. Do likewise with the second finger of your left hand.

7. Dictate scale degrees for other students in the class to play.*

8. If the Christmas Season is approaching, play three Christmas Carols of your own choice. Select them from school or community song books, or collections of carols.

---

*In contrast to the "rule of rows" which decrees that each pitch or number must be represented before the row can start anew, the type of dictation which is suggested here can be quite formless, returning to the same pitch repeatedly if the dictator wishes. The object is to identify scale degrees **quickly.** The same alertness is required of the dictator too, for he must not only call his numbers rapidly but make sure they have been played correctly.

## ✶ 6 ✶

### Minor Scales in Tetrachords

For some time you have been using minor triads. Let us now examine the structure of minor scales. Unlike major scales, which have only one form, minor scales have *three* forms.

The first (and oldest) form is the **pure,** or **natural.** By placing your fingers over the eight white keys in the octave A to A, you will be in position to play the natural form of the A minor scale. This is the *prototype* or pattern for all natural minor scales. Note carefully where the half steps occur. It is this form which determines the key signature of the scale.

If you raise the seventh degree of the scale one half step from G to G♯ you will have the **harmonic** form of the scale. This is the form which is usually used in conventional harmonic progressions and harmony exercises, and thus explains why the dominant triad is always major, and why the $V_7$ chord is the same in both major and minor keys. (The raised leading tone is the third of the dominant triad.) In spite of its extensive use, this sharp is not considered part of the key signature but is always written in as an accidental.

The third form of the minor scale is the **melodic.** In this, not only the seventh degree is raised from G to G♯, but also the *sixth* degree so that F becomes F♯. This second sharp is also written as an accidental and never included in the signature. These accidentals, occurring on the sixth and seventh degrees, are not always sharps; in some keys they could be **double sharps,** and in some keys they would be **naturals.** Could you identify any of these keys?

The three forms of the minor scale then, along with the major scale, are as follows:

### Major and Minor Scale Structure

```
1  2  3 4  5  6  7 8      MAJOR
1  2 3  4  5 6   7  8     PURE MINOR
1  2 3  4  5  6½7  8      HARMONIC MINOR
1  2 3  4  5  6   7 8     MELODIC MINOR
```

*Figure 52.*

You will notice that between the sixth and seventh degrees of the harmonic scale is a step and a half. This is like the "augmented second" which you encountered in a different context in *Club Zara*.

As with the major scale, both the pure and the harmonic minors descend just as they ascend, but the melodic minor traditionally descends in the pure form.

The plus sign over the sixth and seventh degrees of the harmonic and melodic forms is the customary indication that a note is to be raised a half step.

If you place your fingers over the tetrachords of any major scale and then make the changes necessary to form a pure minor scale, you will find that you have had to move only three fingers—those over the third, sixth, and seventh degrees—each of which you lowered a half step. When you construct a harmonic scale you need make only two changes, and when you build a melodic scale you change *only one note!*

To make this structural difference very clear, we will, for the time being, play major and minor scales on the same tonic. For example, we will play C major, then C minor in three forms. We may proceed in dominant, subdominant, or chromatic order, but the major and minor scales will always begin on the same tonic, or keynote.

In theory and harmony courses students frequently are taught to couple minor scales with their **relative** majors (the tonic three half steps higher) because the key signatures are the same*. For pianists, however, coupling the tonic or **parallel** minors with their majors not only makes clearer their structural differences but simplifies fingering problems at a later stage.

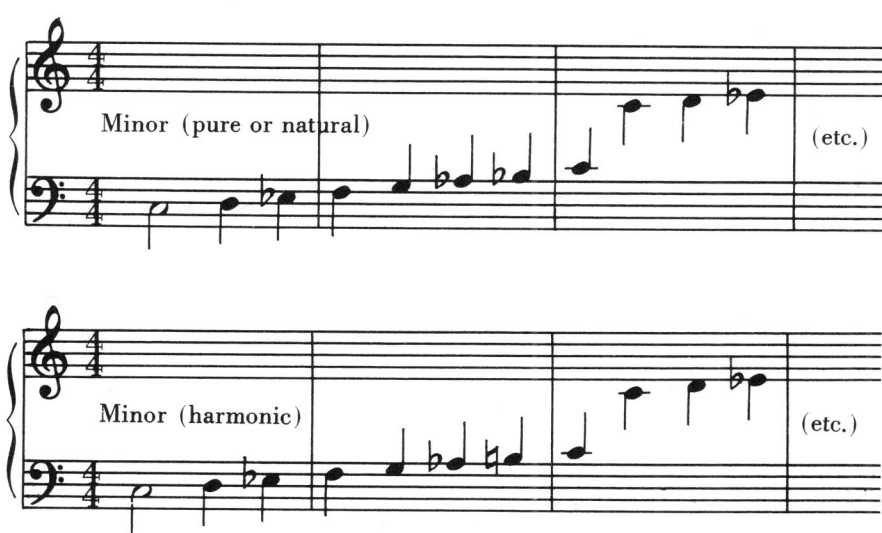

*They are presented this way in the Appendix.

*Figure* 53.

## Transposing the Minor Melodies in Chapter 4

When you are sure of the three forms of the minor scale and can isolate 6 and 7 in any form and in any key, you may return to the songs in Chapter 4 and play them in every minor key. Be sure to determine which of the three forms the song is in and play the tetrachord scale *in that form*. It is a curious fact that although in conventional harmony the harmonic form of the minor scale is regularly used, a significant number of folk-songs and traditional melodies, as well as the works of known composers, are cast in the pure, or natural, form of the minor. To harmonize such melodies one must adopt to a large extent the mode-form implicit in the melody. You will not wish to harmonize the seventh degree of a natural minor scale with a $V_7$ chord, so either leave the tone unharmonized, or consider it an accented passing tone and use a i or iv chord.

## Roots

Like trees, chords have **roots** from which they grow. In our Western traditional system of harmony, chords are constructed by the simple device of superimposing a series of thirds over any given tone which is then considered the chord's root. For example, in your old friend the C major triad, C is the root, E is a third above C, and G is a third above E. We speak of E and G as being the "third" and "fifth" of the triad because they are a third and fifth, respectively, above the root; but the chord is still composed of two thirds—one above the other. In a major triad the lower of the two thirds is major (four half steps) and the upper third is minor (three half steps). In a minor triad the lower third is minor and the upper third is major. In other words, the mode (major or minor) of the triad is determined by the lower third.

## Major and Minor Thirds

In case you are not yet sure of thirds, remember that every third will include three neighboring letter names. The third from C to E includes C, D, E. The third from E to G includes E, F, G. Also, thirds will always be found either on neighboring lines of the staff or in neighboring spaces, so the eye can very easily identify them on the printed page.

It is absolutely essential that you learn to compute intervals by *both* methods — letter names *and* half steps. The letter names will tell you of what *kind* the interval is — second, third, and so on; the number of half steps will tell you its *quality* — major, minor, augmented, and so on. You must also learn to compute intervals from the upper note down as well as from the lower note up.

Bear in mind that although you include the first note when you calculate intervals by letter names, you must not include the first note when you count half steps because what you are calculating here is the *distance from* the first note. Thus, in counting the half steps between C and E, you would proceed as follows:

From **C** to **C♯** is the *first* half step
From **C♯** to **D** is the *second* half step
From **D** to **D♯** is the *third* half step
From **D♯** to **E** is the *fourth* half step

In counting downward from E reverse the process:

From **E** to **E♭** is the *first* half step
From **E♭** to **D** is the *second* half step
From **D** to **D♭** is the *third* half step
From **D♭** to **C** is the *fourth* half step

*Figure 54.*

Identify the thirds in Figure 55, indicating those which are major with a capital M and those which are minor with a small m.

*Figure 55.*

## Triads in Three Positions

We have been playing our tonic triads in what is known as **root position,** that is, with the root positioned as the lowest tone. The three notes of our triad can, however, be regrouped so that a tone other than the root appears at the bottom while the root appears in one of the other parts, or voices. Such rearrangements are called **inversions.** In piano music there are many occasions when the left hand plays the root in the bass (lowest part) while the right hand plays the three notes of the triad in various groupings. We cannot properly call these groupings inversions as long as the root remains in the bass, so we call them **positions.** For the present it will be convenient to call them "positions" even when the left hand is **tacit** (not playing).

Right hand in 1st position;      in 2nd position;      in 3rd position

*Figure* 56.

Notice that whatever its location, C is always the root. Likewise, E is always the third, and G is always the fifth. Can you identify the root, third, and fifth in each of the chords in Figure 57? This rule will help you:

### Rule for Finding the Root of a Chord

**When all the tones of a chord are arranged so that they form a series of thirds, the lowest tone will be the root.**

*Figure* 57.

Play a G Major triad in 2nd position
B Major 3rd
C♯ Major 2nd
B♭ Major 1st
f minor 3rd
a minor 2nd
f♯ minor 1st
e minor 3rd

To help get the feel of these positions with ease and precision, do the following warmup:

WARMUP XIII

Play this through all major and minor keys until you can do it easily hands alone, then play the hands together. Play it also in subdominant and chromatic order.

## Common Tones

If you build a major triad on C (C E G) and then build another major triad on the subdominant (F A C), you will observe that while two of the notes in each triad are different, one is the same — C. This is called the **common tone** because the two chords have this tone in common. One of the first rules of chord progression the student of harmony learns is to **keep the common tone in the same voice and move the other voices to the nearest chord tones.** When both I chord and IV chord are in first position, the two C's are an octave apart, but since C is the common tone it must remain in the voice in which it first appeared (the lowest). To accomplish this we must regroup the notes of the F chord so that C can remain in the lowest voice. The two other notes of the C triad move to the two other notes of the F triad which are nearest them, E moving to F and G moving to A. This will explain the progression I IV I which you learned by rote in Chapter III.

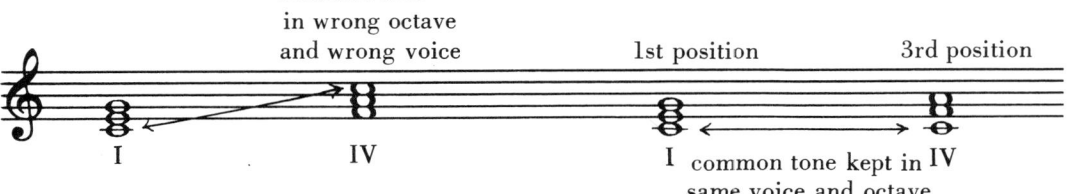

*Figure* 58.

This applies, of course, to all positions of the triads. If we begin with a second position of the C triad, the common tone will still be C, only now it will be in the highest part, or soprano, and there it must remain. If we begin with a C triad in third position, the common tone will be in the alto (middle part) and must stay fixed like the filling in a sandwich. You will notice that the position of the second chord is never the same as that of the first chord.

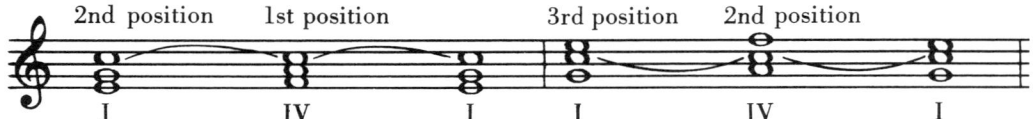

*Figure* 59.

Play I IV I starting from all three positions, in all major and minor keys, and with each hand separately. CAUTION! Remember that when the tonic triad is minor the subdominant triad will also be minor, but before you automatically lower the *middle* tone of the iv chord a half-step, ask yourself which tone *really* is the third.

## The Dominant Triad

Let us now examine the progression I V (not $V_7$).

*Figure* 60.

Here the common tone, G, is in the same octave for both chords, but is *not in the same voice*. In the I chord the G is in the soprano, while in the V chord it is in the tenor (lowest of the three upper parts). We solve the problem by retaining the common tone in the soprano of both chords and moving the two lower voices of the I chord to the nearest tones of the V chord.

You will quickly notice that the V chord in this position (second) is very like the $V_7$ chord which you have been playing by rote, but do not confuse them. In the $V_7$ the third of the I chord moves upward, while in the V the third moves downward.

*Figure* 61.

## Cadences

The progressions V I and IV I are often heard at the end of compositions or sections of compositions and are then called **cadences.** A cadence is a conventional chord progression at the end of a piece or section, designed to give a feeling of rest or finality. The progression IV I is called a **plagal** or **church cadence,** and you hear it in the "A-men" at the conclusion of hymn tunes. V I is an **authentic cadence,** and the combination I IV (I) V I is known as a **complete cadence.**

Here are the three cadences with the upper voices in all three positions. They are written in major mode but you should play them in minor mode as well and in all keys. Just remember that although the subdominant chord follows the mode of the tonic, **the dominant chord is always major.** The connecting lines indicate common tones and should not be read as ties.

CHAPTER SIX 87

*Figure* 62.

## Intervals

By now you are familiar with a number of intervals—half steps, whole steps, thirds, fifths, octaves. Reference has been made to "augmented seconds," and "sevenths" in connection with dominant sevenths. Let us complete our knowledge and formalize it in the schedule at Figure 63.

|  NUMBER OF HALF STEPS | INTERVAL |
|---|---|
| 0 = | **unison** or **perfect prime** |
| 1 = | **minor 2nd** |
| 2 = | **major 2nd** |
| 3 = | **minor 3rd** |
| 4 = | **major 3rd** |
| 5 = | **perfect 4th** |
| ⎡ 6 = | **augmented 4th** |
| ⎣ 6 = | **diminished 5th** |
| 7 = | **perfect 5th** |
| 8 = | **minor 6th** |
| 9 = | **major 6th** |
| 10 = | **minor 7th** |
| 11 = | **major 7th** |
| 12 = | **perfect octave** |

*Figure* 63.

You will have noticed that a number of qualitative words are used to describe the intervals: perfect, major, minor, augmented, diminished. It is frequently said that the major intervals are those which occur in the major scale—counting up from the tonic; the minor intervals are those which occur in the minor scale; the perfect intervals are those which occur in *both* major and minor scales. Immediately you are going to point out that this is all very well for 1, 4, and 5—they do occur in both modes. But what about 2? It also is the same in both modes, yet it is called a "major second." This apparent inconsistency will soon be explained.

The trouble with using this method to establish the identity of intervals is that one always is obliged to consider the lower tone in the interval as the tonic of the key whereas, in context, the lower tone could be *any* degree of the scale. Moreover, counting up becomes the sole means of identifying an interval and the very needful ability to reckon downward is not acquired.

Because of these limitations we shall stress learning intervals by the number of half steps they include, and in this way all intervals will be easily recognizable regardless of context, position in octave, or whether they are calculated upward or downward.

The perfect intervals retain their quality of "perfection" when they are inverted. (Bear in mind that "inverted" only means "upside down.") Thus, a perfect fourth inverts to a perfect fifth; a perfect prime inverts to a perfect octave. On the other hand, major intervals invert to minor, and minor intervals invert to major. This is the reason the interval between 1 and 2 is a major second even though it occurs in both modes: it inverts to a *minor* seventh.

Perhaps you have noticed that the interval and its inversion always total *nine*. A third inverts to a sixth, a fifth to a fourth, and so on.

Also, you may have noticed in the interval schedule the inclusion of **two** intervals, each with six half steps. This is really a matter of spelling. If you count six half steps up from C (see Figure 54) you will arrive at the lowest of the group of three black keys, but, out of context, who is to say if this key is F sharp or G flat? If it is a G flat it will be a fifth up from C because the interval C—G embraces five letter names—C, D, E, F, G. If, however, the key is F sharp the interval will be only a fourth because it embraces only four letter names. In the case of the fifth, the interval is one half step smaller than the perfect fifth, so we say it is **diminished.** In the case of the fourth, the interval is one half step larger than the perfect fourth, therefore we say it is **augmented.**

**All perfect and major intervals may be augmented by adding one half step. All perfect and minor intervals may be diminished by subtracting one half step.**

Figure 64 will make this clear.

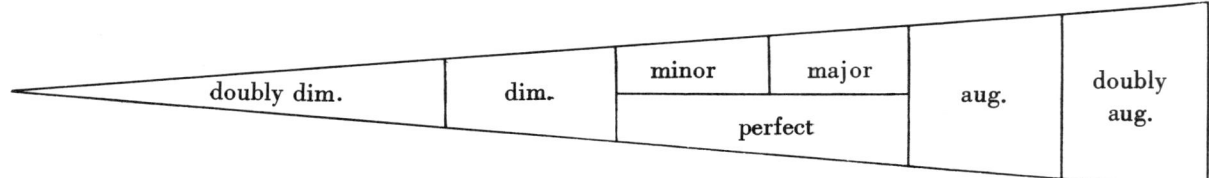

*Figure* 64.

Major intervals may not become diminished; minor intervals may not become augmented. Augmented intervals may become **doubly augmented** by adding another half step; diminished intervals may be **doubly diminished** by subtracting another half step.

In identifying intervals, follow these steps:

1. Determine the kind of interval by counting letter names.
2. Determine its quality by counting half steps as described in Figure 54.
3. Consult the interval schedule. If the number of letter names

and of half steps match a listed interval, you have your answer.

4. If the interval includes one more half step than given in the schedule for the perfect or major interval with the same number of letter names, the interval will be augmented.
5. If the interval includes one less half step than given in the schedule for the perfect or minor interval with the same number of letter names, the interval will be diminished.

For example, C to A sharp is a sixth because it includes six letters, but it has ten half steps—one more than the major sixth in the schedule—therefore it must be an augmented sixth. C sharp to A flat also has six letters but only seven half steps—one less than the minor sixth—therefore it has to be a diminished sixth, even though it sounds like a perfect fifth and has the same number of half steps.

What are the following intervals?

*Figure* 65.

Above and below each note in Figure 66 write notes at the designated intervals. M = major, m = minor, P = perfect, A = augmented, DA = doubly augmented, d = diminished, dd = doubly diminished.

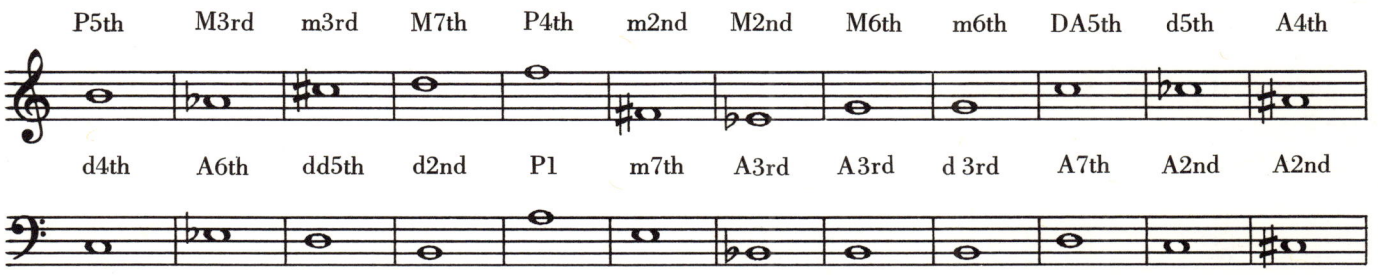

*Figure* 66.

## Accompaniment Patterns

So far we have been harmonizing melodies with chords (**block chords** in which the tones are struck together). Some melodies, particularly those in triple or compound meters, lend themselves to a type of accompaniment in which the tones of the chord are played individually or in different combinations **(broken chords).** Thus, the chord progression I $V_7$ I could be played in the following ways:

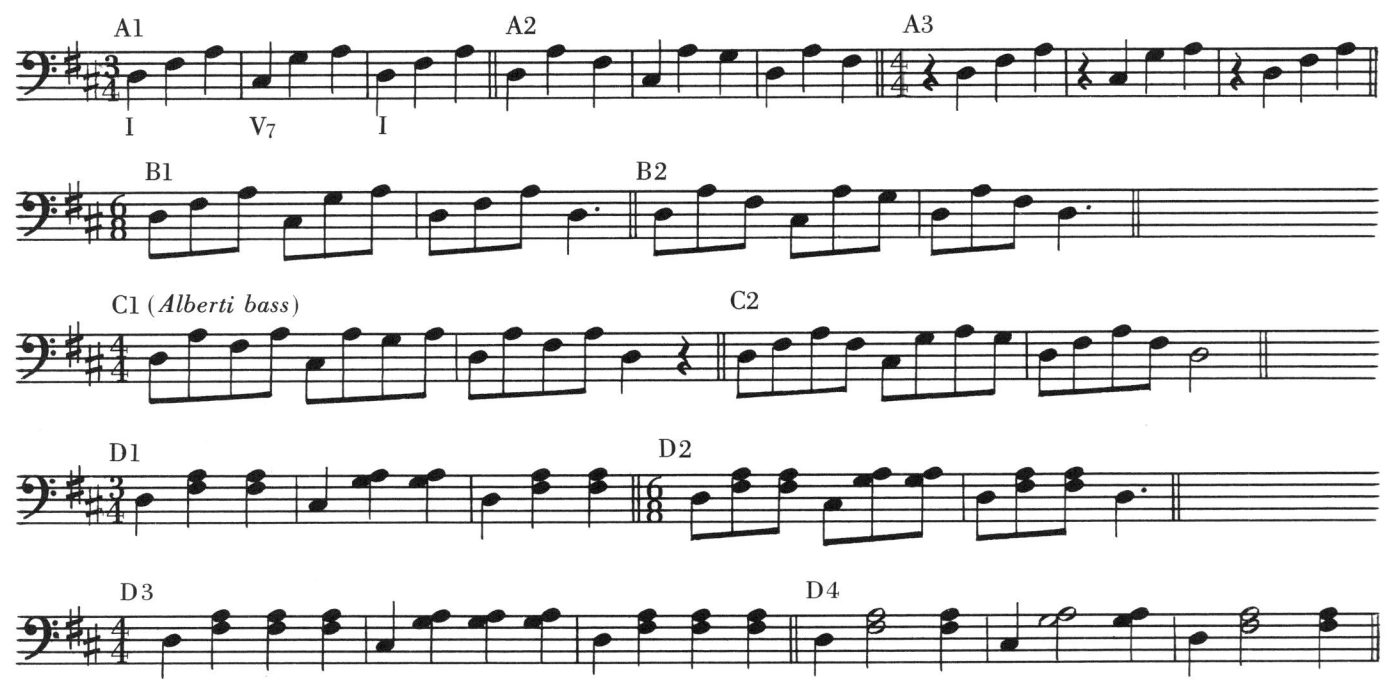

Figure 67.

DID YOU EVER SEE A LASSIE?

German

## WHERE, O WHERE HAS MY LITTLE DOG GONE?

German

These two songs embody a common feature in their melody structure: the second half of each first phrase defines the dominant triad in its root position. The third and fourth measures of *Where, Oh Where Has My Little Dog Gone?* give the complete chord while the third full measure of *Did You Ever See A Lassie?* has only the root and fifth of the V chord, but the force of the dominant harmony is the same.

*Ten Little Indians* shares this same feature—indeed, the entire tune is composed of only the tones of the I and V triads in their root positions. Write the melody in any key you wish, and then add the appropriate harmonies.

Use the new accompaniment patterns to harmonize the melodies in this chapter, then use them to accompany earlier songs and melodies when appropriate.

### WARMUP XIV

Warmup XIV is designed to give individual fingers greater speed and precision in articulation. In each measure hold down silently *all the keys* except the one which is being reiterated. Play both A and B in all major and minor keys, first with the right hand, then with the left.

## WARMUP XV

Warmup XV is another way in which to get the feel of the octave span. We call this **inch worming,** and if you have ever observed an inch worm's method of locomotion you will understand why. Be sure to bring your thumb up to your little finger before stretching your hand out for the next octave on the way up, and on the way down be sure to bring your little finger to your thumb. This is one time when you should *not* keep your hand framed to the octave. Play the warmup on all keys.

**Rhythm Drill**

## Some Basic Principles of Interpretation

Until now your attention has been fully engaged by the complexities of fingers, keys, and chords. Nothing has been said about expression, and expression marks have been kept to a minimum in your music. But some magic beyond accurately ordered sounds is needed to make music come to life, and that magic is **interpretation.**

Since all music disciplines (together with other art forms) are governed by certain general esthetic values, let us restrict our discussion of interpretation to a few practical procedures which relate particularly to piano playing.

1. A good effect is frequently produced by playing louder as a melodic line ascends, and softer as it descends. (Beware of increasing speed during a *crescendo*.)

2. Unless the left hand has the melody, it should play a little softer than the right hand. If the right hand is playing *mezzo forte* (**mf**) the left hand should be playing *mezzo piano* (**mp**). If a *crescendo* occurs in the right-hand part the left hand should also make a crescendo, but always one degree softer.

3. It is usually good practice to taper off or "lighten up" dynamically at the end of a phrase, even when the last note under the slur falls on an accented beat. Slavish accenting of first beats is fine for beginning pianists and marching bands but gives a "squared off" effect to music, while "shaping" the phrase makes the music more supple and eloquent. The same principle applies to two notes slurred together: the second should usually be softer than the first.

4. Generally, a broadening out or slight *ritard* at the end of a composition gives an effect of importance and finality, and, if you are careful not to overdo it, you may hesitate just the least bit before the final note or chord.

5. Think of the music as being horizontal rather than vertical, even in a forest of chords. In good music every note, chord, phrase, or section grows logically out of what preceded it and leads logically to what follows.

6. If a phrase or *motif* is repeated one or more times, try to vary each repetition. You can do this by playing softer or louder, or modifying the time (*rubato*), or varying the touch (*staccato*, *legato*, *portato*), or bringing out an inner voice—to mention a few possibilities.

7. Never "punch," "poke," or "hit" the keys. Try to achieve a "singing tone" by *transferring* the weight of your fingers, hand, and arm from one key to the next in a lateral and gliding motion.

8. Always be aware of left-hand interest. Even when the bass part has a strictly accompanying task, a good composer will try to build in elements of counterpoint, imitation, or rhythmic variety. When you discover such details, highlight them. This is another way in which repetitions may be varied.

9. Bring out the highest notes of right-hand chords.

10. Observe phrasing carefully. If it is not indicated in your music, work it out for yourself. Remember that a phrase is more than a collection of notes which are to be played legato: it is a musical utterance with a specific meaning to communicate. Singing the melody will help you feel where the musical commas and periods should go. Do not feel bound by the phrasing given in your music, but if you change it make sure you have a good reason for doing so. Sometimes the meaning of the music is so clear that no phrasing marks are necessary.

Be careful to make an actual (though slight) break between phrases. Do not content yourself with a mere twitch of the wrist which *looks* effective but permits the last note of one phrase to connect with the first note of the next phrase. You must actually lift your fingers from the keys for an instant and "let the air in." (Sometimes, of course, the last note of one phrase *is* the first note of the next.)

11. Finally, plan your dynamics in advance. Never depend on the inspiration of the moment. If, after careful planning, you *do* feel inspired, your performance will be all the better. Plotting the dynamic scheme of any but the simplest music requires thought and experimentation. When you have decided what you want, mark it in your music.

Most important of all, *listen* to your playing, not just for correct notes and time, but for music—*beautiful* music!

## THE QUEEN'S DOLOUR

Purcell

## BOURLESQ

Leopold Mozart
from his notebook

CHAPTER SIX

## LITTLE ETUDE NO. I

Louis Kohler
1820–1886

## MINUET IN G MAJOR, NO. II

Bach

## MUSETTE

Bach

## CLOUDY DAY

Carl Reinecke
1824-1910

## SPANISH DANCE
(A duet)

McLain

102   CLASS PIANO

Here is some more boogie; the pattern is the one you had in Chapter 4 but now it employs IV and V chords as well as I chords in **root position.**

GASLIGHT BOOGIE

McLain

## Sight-Reading

## Improvisation

By this time you should feel at ease with unaccented passing tones, so let us add another of the non-harmonic tones to our resources—the **chromatic lower neighbor.** This, you may recall from Chapter 5, is the half step below any scale degree, always moving away from and returning to the same tone. It may be a normal degree of the scale as at *b* in Figures 68 and 69, or it may be chromatically raised (sharped or naturaled), as at *a*.

Complete the beginnings, adding measures to make two four-measure phrases. Then improvise your own creations in a predetermined number of measures and phrases.

*Figure 68.*

*Figure 69.*

In Chapter 4 you had a piece called *Pentatonia* which was based on the pentatonic scale. The pentatonic scale is like a major scale with the 4 and 7 omitted, or a pure minor scale with 2 and 6 omitted. It can be played entirely on the five black keys, or any others so long as the same interval structure is preserved. You may start the scale on any of the five tones. There is no true major or minor, but certain combinations give modal effects.

Carry on from the model beginnings, then improvise your own melodies. These may be divided between the hands or played by the two hands simultaneously. Do not harmonize them.

*Figure 70.*

*Figure 71.*

*Figure* 72.

A charming effect can be had by *group improvisation* on the pentatonic scale. To do this, everyone plays at random on the black keys of the two highest octaves, *as softly as possible.* You will hear a Westerner's idea of pagoda bells.

## ✷ Hearsay and Other Ear Work

1. Play a note on the piano and sing a pitch a major third higher; a minor third higher; a major third lower; a minor third lower.
2. Identify major and minor thirds as someone else plays them.
3. Identify the positions of triads as someone else plays them.
4. Identify plagal, authentic, and complete cadences as someone plays them. Tell whether they are major or minor and which chord tone is in the soprano.
5. Identify the three forms of the minor scale as someone plays them up and down one octave.
6. Play the first five tones of a minor scale and sing 6, 7, 8, in the pure form. Do the same in the harmonic and melodic forms—always *after* playing the first five tones.
7. As someone plays the five tones of a pentatonic scale (on black keys), identify the first note.
8. As your teacher, or a fellow student, plays songs and pieces—sometimes observing phrasing, sometimes not—raise your hand when you hear a phrase properly played.
9. Play and harmonize *Oh, Dear, What Can the Matter Be?* and *Ten Little Indians* by ear, and in all keys.

## ⋆ Review and Suggested Assignments

1. Define the following terms:
   pure minor scale; natural minor scale; harmonic minor scale; melodic minor scale; tonic minor scale; parallel minor scale; relative minor scale; root; major third; minor third; root position; doubled; tacit; first position; second position; third position; third (of triad); fifth (of triad); soprano; common tone; alto; cadence; authentic cadence; plagal cadence; complete cadence; voice leading; block chords; triple time; compound time; diminished; augmented; perfect (of an interval); inverted; broken chords; accidental.

2. Play notes a major third and a minor third above and below each key in an octave.

3. Construct major and minor triads in first, second, and third position on all keys in an octave.

4. Play major triads in second and third positions and lower the thirds to make them minor.

5. Play I IV I through all major and minor keys with three voices in the right hand and the roots (single notes) in the left hand.

6. Play I V I, then I $V_7$ I (the right hand starting with first position only) in all major and minor keys, and compare the progression of parts.

7. Play I V I through all major and minor keys in all positions and in all orders with the right hand alone.

8. Proceed as above and double the roots in the bass (left hand).

9. Select an appropriate accompaniment for *Silent Night* and transpose the song into all keys.

10. Harmonize *Oh Dear, What Can the Matter Be?* first with block chords, then with broken chords, and transpose into all keys.

11. Construct minor tetrachord scales in three forms on every note in an octave. First play the scales up and down one octave, then two or more octaves.

12. Write *Ten Little Indians*—melody and chords—in any key but C major.

# ✶ 7 ✶

## Standard Scale Fingering

To be a good musician you are not required to play scales with virtuosity, or even to know standard scale fingering, as long as you are on such good terms with the scales themselves that you can play chords and melodies easily in every key. But to be a good *pianist* it is important for you to play scales and to master the standard fingering so that it becomes automatic. This is because so much keyboard music contains scale passages and because the practice of scales is one of the best ways in which to gain control of fingers.

Folklore would have it that the greater the number of sharps or flats in a key, the more difficult is that scale to play. Actually, the reverse is true: the more black keys in a scale, the easier it is to play. Any skilled pianist will tell you that the scale of C major is the most difficult of all.

Accordingly, we are going to begin with those scales which include all five black keys. These are the keys which have five or more sharps or flats—B major, F♯ major, C♯ major, and their enharmonic equivalents, C♭ major, G♭ major, D♭ major—and we shall call them **Group I.** In all these scales the group of three black keys will be played by the three middle fingers, and the two black keys will be played by the two fingers nearest the thumb—2 and 3. There will be only two white keys in each octave and these will be played by the thumb.

We will play the scale of C♯ major first, and we will play the *black* keys in *clusters* rather than individually. Thus, we will play C♯ and D♯ *together*.

*Figure* 73.

After you have played this with each hand alone two or three times, play it hands together, up and down one octave. After that play two octaves. Be sure to give two counts to each impact. Now play the notes individually (you can probably do this hands together). Stopping for two counts on each tonic is good procedure for a while as it gives you a chance to think ahead, but give the other scale degrees only one count as you did when you played the scales in tetrachords.

Now you have played the scale of C♯—*seven sharps*—with the greatest of ease.

The scale of F♯ major is just as easy. Only one tone is different—B instead of B♯—and of course this time we will start with the group of three black keys played as a cluster. Proceed just as you did with the scale of C♯ major.

The scale of B major starts on a white key, so play the tonic with your thumbs and continue as you did in the other scales. When you are quite sure of the fingering pattern for B major you may make two changes—**replacements** which enable you to begin the scale with the fourth finger of your left hand and play the highest B with the fifth finger of your right hand. Doing this makes the fingering a bit more "pianistic," but if it confuses you at all, continue using your thumb on B.

A simple rule will help you to remember the fingering for minor scales: major scales starting on white keys and their *tonic* minors will be fingered alike; major scales starting on black keys and their *relative* minors, provided they too start on black keys, will be fingered alike.

Only the scales of C♯ major and F♯ major have relative minors on black keys. Be very careful to preserve the fingering pattern in the various forms of the minor. When you feel quite sure of the fingering you may use another replacement: the right hand may begin both of these scales with the *second* finger instead of the third in the scale of D♯ minor, and the fourth in the scale of A♯ minor. But again, if this tends to confuse you, do not do it.

Since the scale of B major begins on a white key its *tonic* minor will be fingered in the same way.

Although the scales of F major and F minor do not include all of the black keys, they too are governed by the Group I fingering pattern so that both thumbs are played on F and C. The only replacement occurs when the highest F is played by the *fourth* finger (not thumb) of the right hand, and the lowest F is played by the fifth finger of the left hand.

# VENERABLE CLASSIC
(A duet)

Traditional
Arranged by M. S. McLain

CHAPTER SEVEN 113

## Strumming

Pianists sometimes have occasion to provide for instrumentalists or group singers an accompaniment which does not include the melody. One of the most usual and useful of such accompaniments is **strumming.** The hands alternate for this, the left hand playing the root or some other chord tone as a single note or octave and the right hand supplying the harmony. This kind of accompaniment is capable of many variations. Figures 74 through 77 show four possibilities. The first two employ only the chord roots in the bass; the last two alternate the roots with the fifths.

Observe that the fifth of the dominant is the second degree of the scale (the supertonic), while the fifth of the subdominant is the tonic. Thus, the only scale degrees which you will be using in the bass are:

- I, which is the root of the tonic and the fifth of the subdominant.
- II, which is the fifth of the dominant.
- IV, which is the root of the subdominant.
- V, which is the root of the dominant and fifth of the tonic.

This type of accompaniment is best adapted to melodies whose harmony remains the same throughout one or more measures. If, as in a cadence, the harmony does change on each beat, the hands may be temporarily played *together* in conformity with the harmony suggested by the melody.

We have designated as **plain strumming** that in which only the roots appear in the bass. Figure 74 and Figure 75 show how I, $V_7$, and IV chords can be strummed in this way. When we alternate roots and fifths we become **fancy.** Figure 76 gives a I $V_7$ I IV sequence, and Figure 77 the type of pattern you could find in many songs. On the last count of the next-to-the-last measure a $V_7$ chord could be used in place of the tonic triad if the melody called for it.

Which pattern does the *secondo* part of *Venerable Classic* follow?

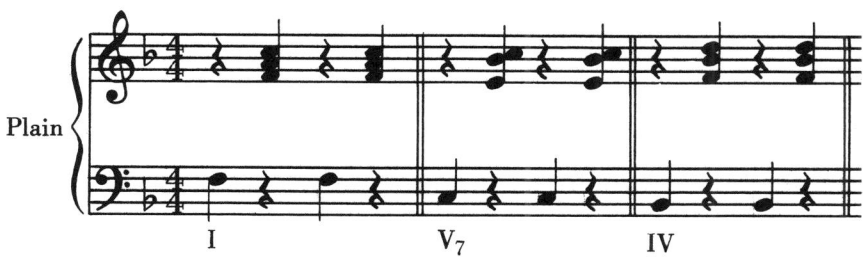

*Figure* 74.

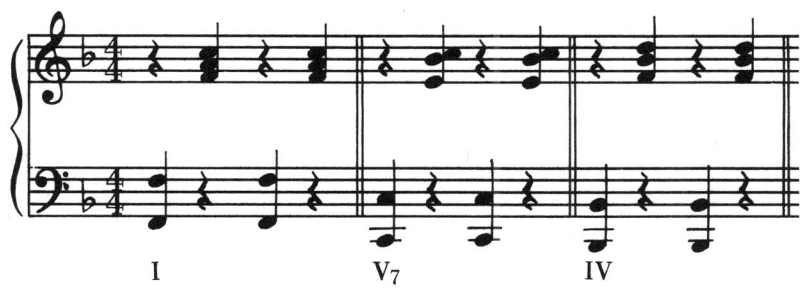

*Figure* 75.

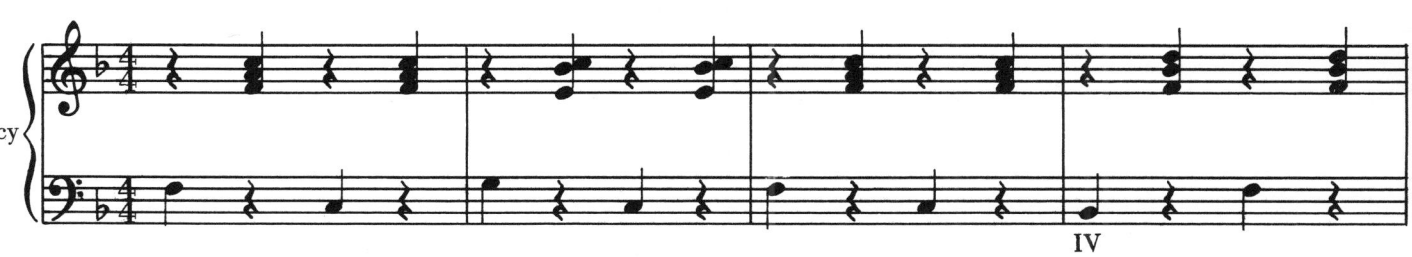

*Figure* 76.

*Figure 77.*

## Songs for Strumming

### CLEMENTINE

P. Montrose

### POLLY WOLLY DOODLE

American

### LONG, LONG AGO

T. H. Bayly
1797–1839

Make duets of your earlier songs, strumming the *secondo* part.

Sometimes we find a change of key in the course of a melody. *Little Minka* has eight measures in A minor, then four measures in the relative major (C) followed by a return to A minor for four measures. You can harmonize it with block chords on the first count of each measure, and you can strum to it in duet style, plain or fancy, using either quarter or eighth notes.

Reviewing Warmup VI will help you with the minor-major-minor chord changes.

### LITTLE MINKA

Russian

## More Left-hand Accompaniments

The device of alternating root and fifth in the lowest voice or bass of an accompaniment is not limited to strumming but may be used in accompaniments for the left hand alone. Which of the patterns in Figure 78 can you adapt to the new songs? The meters, note-values and sequence of harmonies may all be modified, of course, to suit the melody.

CHAPTER SEVEN

*Figure* 78.

Which of your other songs would be improved by this more varied style of accompaniment? Examples of appropriate matings would be: b. with *Lavender's Blue*; c. with *Where, Oh Where Has My Little Dog Gone?*; g. with *Silent Night*.

### Inversions

As you learned in Chapter 6, when a chord tone other than the root is in the bass, the chord is said to be **inverted.** When the third of the chord is in the bass the chord is in its **first inversion;** when the fifth of the chord is in the bass the chord is in its **second inversion.**

When the chord is in root position (root in the bass) the triad is referred to as a **five-three** chord because the other tones are a fifth and a third above the bass. In accordance with this logic, the first inversion is referred to as a **six-three** chord because the upper tones are a sixth and a third above the bass, and the second inversion is a **six-four** chord because the upper tones form a sixth and a fourth above the bass.

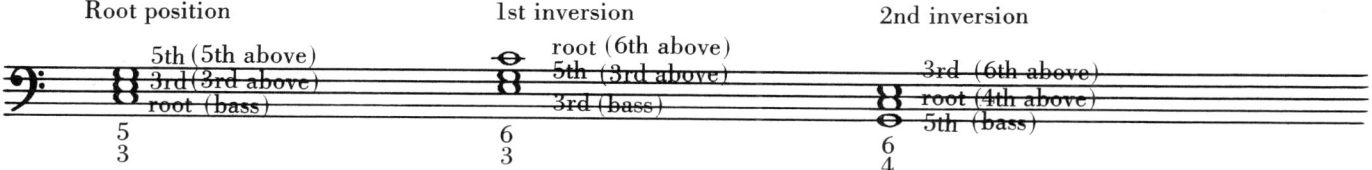

*Figure* 79.

When these same groupings of the chord tones occurred in the upper three voices we called them **positions** (Triads in Three Positions, Chapter 6) because it is possible for them all to occur over a stationary root in the bass. Thus, first, second, and third positions could all be different aspects of *root* position—or of first inversion—or of second inversion.

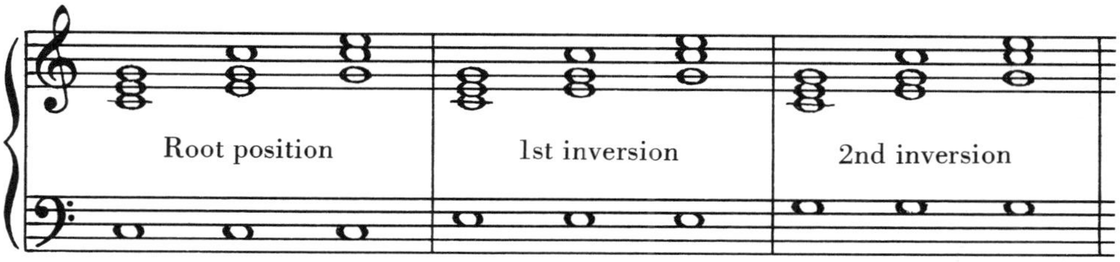

*Figure* 80.

Identify the $^5_3$, $^6_3$, and $^6_4$ chords in Figure 81. You will have no difficulty if you first locate the root of each chord as you learned to do in Chapter 6. Having located the root, you can easily identify the third and fifth.

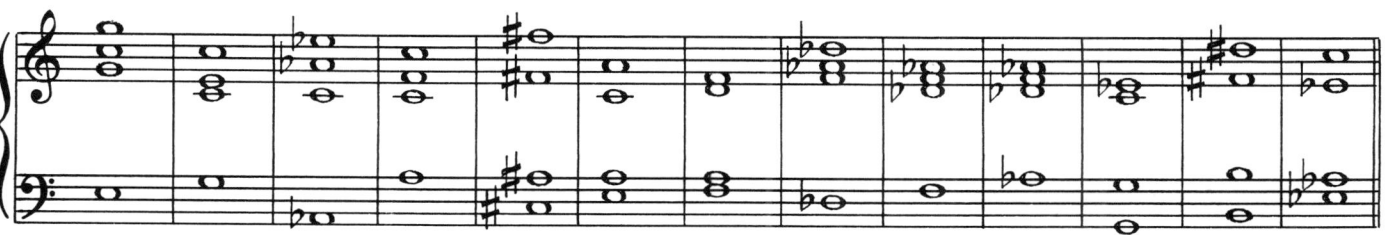

*Figure* 81.

When, in fancy strumming, you alternate the root and fifth of a chord with your left hand, you are playing alternate $^5_3$ and $^6_4$ chords.

Generally an **unfigured** bass note is assumed to be the root of the chord and the figures (5 and 3), being understood, are omitted. In the first inversion, the 3 of the $^6_3$ is understood and so omitted. Only the second inversion is expressed by two figures, $^6_4$.

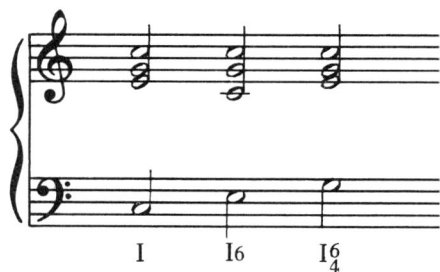

Figure 82.

$I^6_4$ chords are frequently used in cadences where they are called **cadential six-fours.** Let us go back to Chapter 6 and reexamine the first authentic cadence in Figure 62. There we had I V I with roots in the bass. If we now replace the first bass C with a G (fifth of the chord) we will have a $I^6_4$ V I.

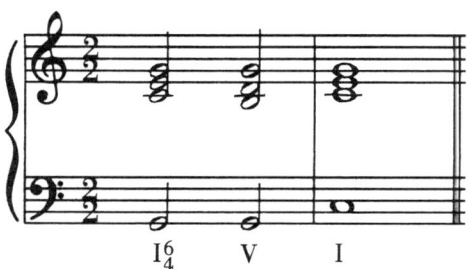

Figure 83.

Play authentic cadences in all major and minor keys, substituting a cadential $I^6_4$ for the first tonic chord.

Now let us consider complete cadences. The third chord, which has been a tonic triad in root (or **fundamental**) position, may now be converted to a $I^6_4$ merely by leading the bass up a whole step from the subdominant to the dominant. The note may be repeated in the same octave as root of the dominant which follows, or it may move an octave lower—whichever sounds better or is more convenient.

Just make sure to lead the bass *one whole step up* from IV to V, never a seventh down or an eleventh up.

*Figure* 84.

Play complete cadences (as in Figure 84) in all major and minor keys, and with the upper voices in all positions. After you have played the cadences with block chords, play them with broken chords, and then strum them in $\frac{2}{4}$, $\frac{3}{4}$, and $\frac{4}{4}$ time.

*Figure* 85.

The $I_4^6$ need not be preceded or followed by other harmonies; it can follow a I chord in root position and return to it as in Figure 86, or in the *secondo* part of *Venerable Classic*, or, if the left hand is accompanying a right-hand melody, as in Figure 87.

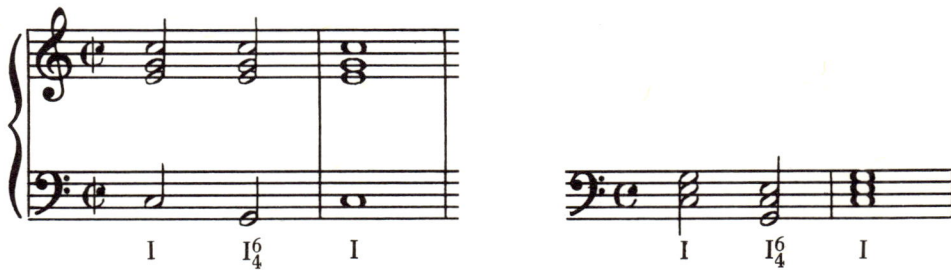

*Figure* 86.                                              *Figure* 87.

CHAPTER SEVEN   121

For the present you will not have occasion to use the $_3^6$ chord as much as the $_4^6$ chord, but there are two ways in which you will encounter it and use it. Both ways involve the first inversion of the IV chord—the IV$_6$.

1. The third of the IV chord may substitute for the fifth of the IV chord in the bass line in fancy strumming. In the *secondo* part of *Venerable Classic* a IV$_6$ is used in two places. Can you find them? By using the third of the IV chord the bass is able to achieve a smoother, less angular line than is possible when it is restricted to the root and the fifth of IV.

2. A IV$_6$ frequently precedes a I$_4^6$ or a V$_7$. For the left hand accompanying a right-hand melody, the progressions would be as shown in Figure 88 and Figure 89.

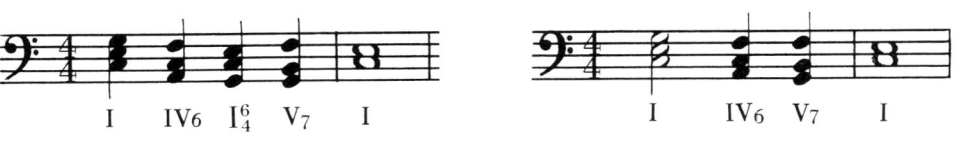

*Figure* 88.                                                   *Figure* 89.

You will notice that the V$_7$ in these examples is different from the V$_7$ which you have been playing, although the notes which comprise it are the same. Actually it is the root position of the chord (fifth omitted) and follows a I$_4^6$ more naturally than the position (an inversion) with which you are familiar.

In Chapter 9 we will consider seventh chords and their inversions in detail, so for the moment it will suffice to learn this progression and its V$_7$ by rote.

You will also notice that in the I chord to which the V$_7$ resolves, the fifth has been omitted. This is because of the strong tendency of the fourth degree of the scale to resolve downward to the mediant. To account for the three voices, the root is considered doubled by bass and tenor.

This gives us three new chord patterns—two incorporating the cadential I$_4^6$, and one bypassing it but using a IV$_6$.

    1.    I    I$_4^6$    V$_7$    I

    2.    I    IV$_6$    I$_4^6$    V$_7$    I

    3.    I    IV$_6$    V$_7$    I

The first pattern can be used in the *Theme from Freischütz*, in *Reuben, Reuben*, and in *Old MacDonald*, which you may first play by ear, then write out and harmonize. Among the older songs it can be used in *Silent Night; Sleep Baby, Sleep; Rosa;* and *Pop Goes the Weasel.*

The second pattern can be used in *Good Night, Ladies* and *The Arkansas Traveler*. A number of earlier songs will be improved by this chord sequence. Among them are *Yankee Doodle; Auld Lang Syne; Lavender's Blue; Oh, Susannah; He's a Jolly Good Fellow; Twinkle, Twinkle;* and *Theme from the Ninth Symphony.*

The third pattern can be used in *Yankee Doodle; Theme from the Ninth Symphony; Rousseau's Lullaby; This Old Man.*

### REUBEN, REUBEN

William Gooch

### GOOD NIGHT, LADIES

E. P. Christy

### THEME FROM FREISCHÜTZ

Carl Maria von Weber
1786–1826

CHAPTER SEVEN

## THE ARKANSAS TRAVELER

American

## Modulating Up One Half Step

Here we must consider one more aspect of the $V_7$ chord; not a new position this time but a new function. Instead of being used in a cadence it is used to *usher in a new key*—in this case, the key one half step higher. This is known as **modulation,** a subject we shall consider in greater detail a little later. At the moment let us simply learn this useful operation by rote. To modulate from C major to $D^\flat$ major, you will play:

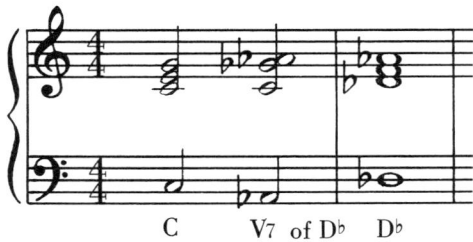

*Figure* 90.

As you can see in Figure 90, this magical modulatory $V_7$ is merely the $V_7$ of the new key, with the dominant of the new key (which is also the root of the $V_7$) in the bass. But for the present it will be quicker and easier to remember how each voice progresses—the bass down a major third (four half steps), the tenor remaining in the same place, the alto moving up a whole step (spelled a diminished third to be consistent with the key of $D^\flat$), and the soprano moving up a half step.

Now modulate by half step through all keys, using this pattern. See if you can discover the pattern for modulating from major to minor, minor to minor, minor to major, remembering always that the $V_7$ invariably will be the same, whatever the mode.

Our first use of this modulatory $V_7$ will be in the second-ending measure of the *Venerable Classic*. The measure was left blank in the *secondo* part so that you could write in the $V_7$ which will take you from C♯ major to D major. Write it as a dotted half-note chord.

So now, in the *Venerable Classic*, you have been introduced to strumming, to $IV_6$ chords, and to modulatory $V_7$'s. The *secondo* part has yet another feature to which your attention is called: in two measures unaccented passing-tones have been introduced in the accompaniment thus giving the bass a more melodic or contrapuntal character. Can you identify these passing tones?

Play the second half of the *secondo* part in all major keys to familiarize yourself with these features. If you wish to experiment with minor mode, try *primo* and *secondo* parts in both harmonic and melodic forms.

In transposing the *primo* part, you will find a solid knowledge of scales absolutely essential. Also, there are places where short-term memorizing can be of help. For example, in the second half of the *primo*, the two voices of the melody move down diatonically in thirds from 1 and 3 to 3 and 5, then back to 1 and 3, and down again to 3 and 5. In such cases it is far easier (and therefore quicker) to remember where you came from and return there than to calculate all over again which notes are 1 and 3 and which are 3 and 5.

## WARMUP XVI

Our new warmup is a **trill** exercise. The cluster of whole notes at the beginning must be **depressed silently** and held for the duration of each new finger combination. Invert for left hand.

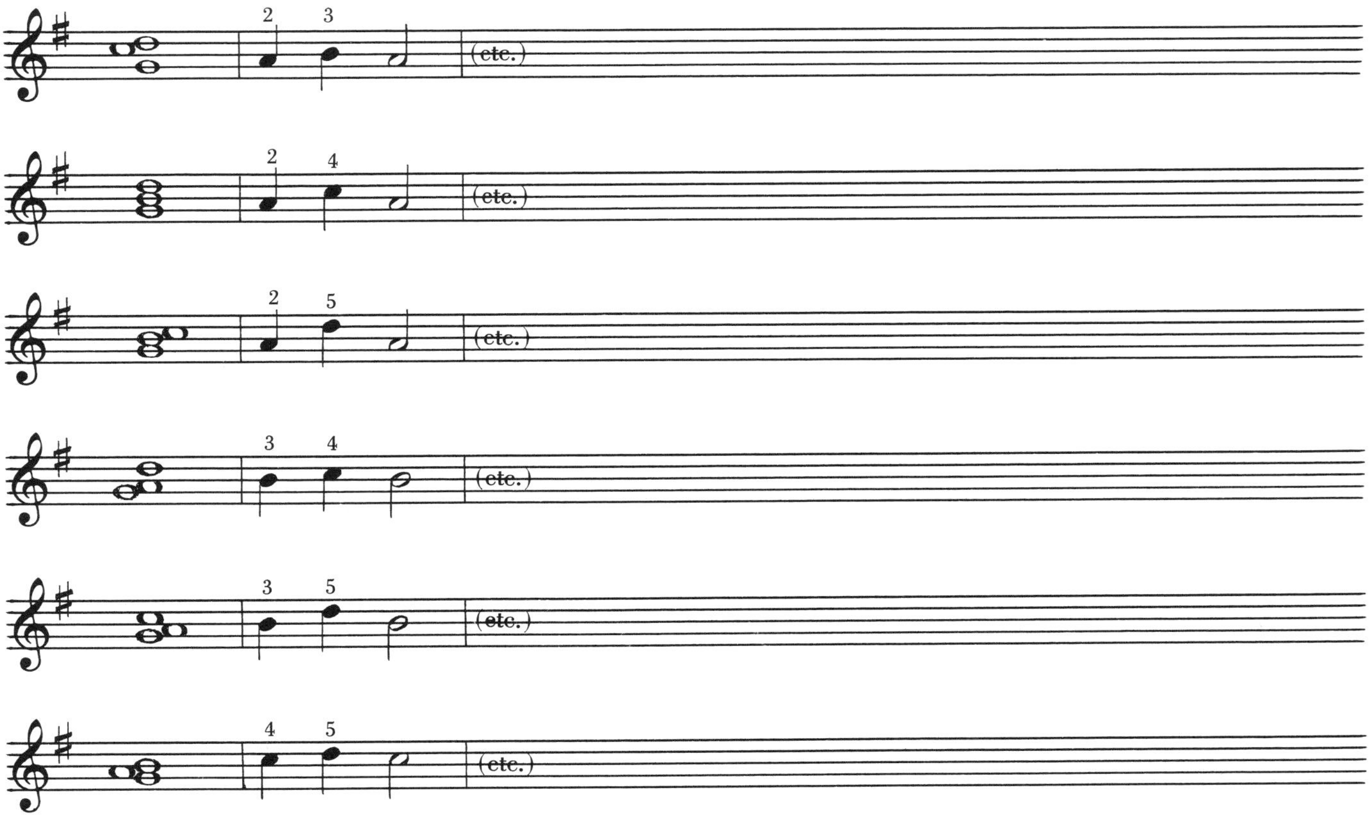

## WARMUP XVII

Warmup XVII is a stretching exercise. If your hands are large and limber you may not need it, but if your hands are small or the muscles are tight and keep you from spreading your fingers comfortably in extended hand positions, this will help. Play slowly and be sure to stop if or when your hand feels any strain. Invert for left hand.

## WARMUP XVIII

Warmup XVIII is to help you gain control of dynamic levels. Watch the *diminuendo* carefully so as not to decrease too abruptly. This principle of graduated increase and decrease of volume may be applied to a number of other warmups as well as to songs and solos.

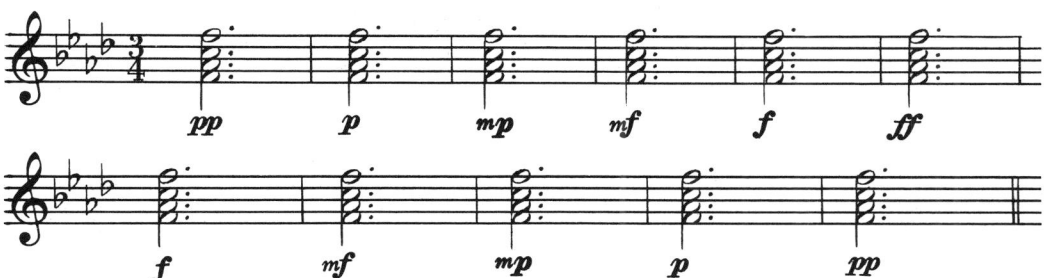

# Rhythm Drill

## Some Basic Principles of Pedaling

Grand pianos and some uprights have three pedals. The pedal at the right is the **damper** or **legato pedal.** It is often mistakenly called the "loud" pedal. This is incorrect because the pedal has nothing to do with loudness. When it is depressed it raises the **dampers** so that they do not touch the strings. This permits all the strings to vibrate freely, not only in response to the hammerstroke on individual strings, but in response to each other. These "open" or unstopped strings set up a resonance of overtones which, used with skill and discrimination, can enhance the pianist's performance, but if used carelessly will produce not loudness but confusion.

The middle pedal on grand pianos also controls the dampers but with this difference: whereas the damper pedal lifts all the dampers at once, the middle or **sostenuto pedal** controls only one or a predetermined few dampers, depending on which keys are being held down at the instant the pedal is depressed. Thus, it is not only selective, but for as long as it is held down will continue to sustain those tones—and those alone—no matter what is played subsequently.

If there is a middle pedal on an upright piano, it is usually not a sostenuto pedal. Sometimes it is a "practice" pedal, which means that it removes the hammers from contact with the strings, making it possible to play soundlessly. Sometimes the pedal is there only for looks and has no function at all. And sometimes, especially in elderly instruments, whatever its original purpose, it long ago retired from active duty.

The pedal at the left is the **soft pedal** and, as its name implies, it decreases the volume of sound. In a grand piano this is accomplished by moving the entire **action** (the mechanical complex in which the hammers are fixed) to the right so that only two strings are struck by the hammers instead of three strings. In an upright piano, approximately the same result is obtained by moving the hammers closer to the strings or by interposing some substance between the hammers and the strings.

Both damper and soft pedals should be used for specific purposes and color effects. Learn to play *legato* without the damper pedal and *piano* without the soft pedal, then when you need extra help the pedals will be your valuable tools.

In Warmup IV (Chapter 3) you used the damper pedal so that you might enjoy the rich sonorities developing from triads played in each octave of the keyboard. However connectedly you might have played these triads you could never, with only your two hands, have compounded the same sonority. Therefore, to achieve this result the damper pedal was indispensable.

There are other special effects, among them legato skips and chords, which necessitate use of the damper pedal. One purpose for which it must *not* be used is "keeping time." Good pedaling demands a high degree of coordination between foot, hands, and ear, and this can never be developed if the foot is restricted to timekeeping.

Two general principles which should guide you are:

1. Change the pedal when the harmony changes.
2. Release the pedal if you make a mistake.

There are two basic kinds of pedaling.

The first we call **direct pedaling.** Here the pedal and key are activated at the same time. This is what you did in the *secondo* part of *Venerable Classic*, and also in the Rhythm Drill in Chapter 4. This type of pedaling adds brilliance to the music and is used in some waltzes, marches, and other pieces where a pronounced rhythm is more important than a sustained melodic line. With direct pedaling it is impossible to play a series of chords legato (unless they are all of the same harmony) for the obvious reason that if the pedal is to be played *with* a chord it must be released in advance and so cause a hiatus between chords. This is the easiest kind of pedaling and the least used by good pianists.

The second kind is **syncopated pedaling.** This is more subtle, more difficult, and more frequently used. In the last three exercises of this chapter's Rhythm Drill you were doing syncopated pedaling. This is for legato, singing melodies, and chord sequences. Here you must depress the pedal immediately *after* striking the note or chord and hold it down until *after* you have played the new harmony, when you will lift and depress the pedal again as rapidly as possible. Actually there is an overlapping of harmonies, but the up-down action of the foot **(pedal change)** is so rapid that the ear does not detect any blur and the effect is one of smoothness—the more so since by lifting and depressing the pedal *after* the key stroke, the overtone resonance resulting from *simultaneous* pedal and key action is eliminated.

*Figure* 91.

Many considerations will influence your choice of pedaling—the period and the composer, for example, and current attitudes toward the period and the composer. There is a continuing controversy over the use of pedal in the keyboard music of J. S. Bach. On the one side it is asserted that because there were no modern pedals on the instruments for which he composed, none should be used today. On the other side it is argued that the spirit and intent of the music are not necessarily best served by slavish adherence to the mechanical limitations of the day. It is pointed out that many composers strained against these same limitations, and the question is raised as to whether, in the name of authenticity, their works should always be thus circumscribed.

It is an interesting debate and you must make your own decision. In any event, good taste would suggest using the pedal sparingly and with utmost clarity in music of the Baroque and Classical periods.

Of a quite different texture and period are those works which introduce the whole-tone scale. There are only two of these scales — on C and D♭. One of their peculiarities is that all of the tones of either one may be considered as a *single* harmony and combined in one pedal. In some contexts you might not want to do this, but in any event you *must* change pedal when one scale complex changes to the other.

Then there is the matter of piano register. If you are playing *forte* in the lower octaves, even though the harmony does not change you are likely to build up a reverberation which is unpleasant, so a judicious change of pedal is indicated. On the other hand, if you are playing a rapid pianissimo passage in the highest register, holding the pedal through changing harmonies often gives a shimmering effect and the theoretical dissonance is scarcely noticeable. In fact, the very highest strings have no dampers so what you do with the pedal affects them not at all.

As with notation, terminology, and many other aspects of music, pedaling is full of inconsistencies to which the professional pianist is accustomed but which are confusing to beginning pianists.

One of these is the matter of pedaling the first beat of a waltz bass and holding the pedal through almost three beats. You did this in *Venerable Classic* if you used pedal. The first beat was a quarter

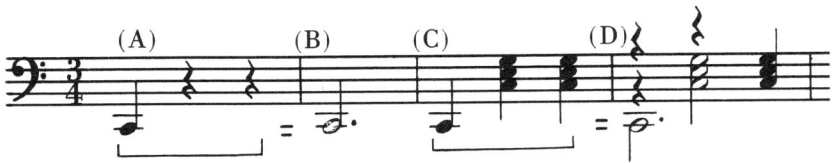

*Figure* 92.

note, which was followed by two quarter rests (A), but the pedal has prolonged that quarter note to almost a dotted half (B). Having been urged to respect rests you now ask, "What is the rationale of this?" Well, there really isn't any. The first note could have been written as a dotted half, and sometimes is. But to be strictly logical, a note on the second beat (C) should be a half note (or a double-dotted quarter) and sundry fill-in rests would be involved, (D) all of which looks fussy and confusing, so it has become a convention to write three quarters and a pedal indication. Like most conventions, this one serves a purpose but wilts a bit in the glare of logic.

Another practice which puzzles students is the use of pedal when the music is marked staccato. The explanation is that the use of a staccato touch—particularly the vigorous pizzicato type—produces a characteristic **timbre** which is not obscured by use of the pedal. A properly performed staccato would never be taken for legato even though the sounds are carried on by the pedal.

One more puzzle: should use of the pedal be geared to the left hand or the right hand? This depends on the function of each hand. Usually the two are coordinated so that no choice need be made. If in more intricate music this problem arises, think first of the melodic line regardless of the hand to which it is assigned. The pedal does not automatically belong with the bass or accompaniment. (One exception is in duets, when the *secondo* player has charge of pedaling.)

Pedaling traditionally is indicated by the abbreviation *Ped.* at the place to be pedaled, and an asterisk, *, where the pedal is to be released. More recently, the mark └──────┘ is gaining favor. This has the advantage of greater precision where intricate pedaling is required. In └─────∧─────∧─────┘ there can be no doubt where the rapid pedal change is to take place since this is an exact diagram of your foot action.

Use of the soft pedal is indicated by the words *una corda* where the pedal is to be depressed, and *tre corde* where it is to be released.

There are two virtuoso techniques which you may not wish to use, but might like to know about: the **trill pedal** in which the foot rapidly flutters the damper pedal up and down to reduce the volume and duration of sounds without the abruptness of a pedal release, and the **half-pedal** in which the damper pedal is depressed only halfway for special effects such as soft bell or chime-like music in the upper registers.

In using the pedal, keep your heel firmly on the floor and your toes pointed straight forward on the pedal. When the pedal is released it should be *fully* released; the slightest depression will cause a blur. On the other hand, never lift your foot higher than the pedal; always keep in contact. The reason for this is that if you let your foot lose contact the sound of the mechanism is apt to result from the pedal release, while your foot's return to the pedal is more than likely to produce an audible tap.

Finally: it is better to use too little pedal than too much.

## Sight-Reading

Before playing these sight-reading exercises, examine them carefully and ask yourself of each one:

1. What key is it in, and do I know this signature?
2. Does it change key, and if so, to what key?

3. Is the motion scalewise or chordwise? (Pay particular attention to those groups of eighth notes which constitute broken chords.)
4. Should my hands cover a five-finger position or an octave span? (Check your left hand as well as your right hand.)
5. Are any harmonies other than the familiar ones employed?
6. What tempo would be appropriate to the music?

When you have found answers to all these questions, try to hear the music in your mind's ear. Then, play it at a tempo which seems appropriate, and keep going—even if you are obliged to leave out a note here and there the first time through. By the third time it should be perfect.

## Improvisation

In Chapter 6 you were introduced to broken chords and other types of accompaniment which you may now use in improvising. Your vocabulary still will consist of I, IV, V, and $V_7$ chords, their individual chord tones, unaccented passing tones, and chromatic lower neighbors—in major and minor (all forms) keys. The melody may exceed an octave by one or two notes at either end if such extension serves your purpose. Greater variety will be achieved through use of the new, more flexible accompaniments. Develop the model beginnings into balanced phrases, then originate your own beginnings and proceed as before.

*Figure 93.*

*Figure 94.*

CHAPTER SEVEN

Figure 95.

The triads in three positions and the cadences which you had in Chapter 6 suggest another style of improvisation. Here the right hand combines melody *and* harmony while the left hand plays single-note roots. In the model beginnings the three upper voices move freely from one position to another *of the same harmony*, skipping intermediate positions to conform to the melody. The first sight-reading study in Chapter 6, and *The Three Horns* in this chapter are written in this style, although they employ more advanced harmonic resources than are presently available to you.

Figure 96.

Figure 97.

# CARNIVAL

François Couperin
1668-1733

## SONATINA, OP. 36, NO. 1
(First Movement)

Muzio Clementi
1752–1832

CHAPTER SEVEN 139

# SPINNING SONG

Anton Ellmenreich

## THE THREE HORNS
(for the left hand alone)

M. S. McLain

142 CLASS PIANO

# AMERICA
(in the key of G major)

Attributed to Henry Carey
1690–1743

# THE STAR-SPANGLED BANNER
(in the key of A flat major)

J. S. Smith

### ★ Hearsay and Other Ear Work

1. Having established the tonality of a given key by playing the scale up and down slowly, identify random scale degrees as they are played for you.
2. Play a note on the piano in your voice range and sing:

   a major third and a perfect fifth higher
   a minor third and a perfect fifth higher
   a minor third and a minor sixth higher
   a major third and a major sixth higher
   a perfect fourth and a major sixth higher
   a perfect fourth and a minor sixth higher

   a major third lower and a minor third higher
   a minor third lower and a major third higher
   a minor third lower and a perfect fourth higher
   a major third lower and a perfect fourth higher
   a perfect fourth lower and a major third higher
   a perfect fourth lower and a minor third higher

a minor third and a perfect fifth lower
a major third and a perfect fifth lower
a minor third and a minor sixth lower
a major third and a major sixth lower
a perfect fourth and a minor sixth lower
a perfect fourth and a major sixth lower.
3. Identify each of the chords you have just sung.
4. As the teacher plays isolated four-part chords, listen to the bass part and identify each chord as being in root position, first inversion, or second inversion.
5. Play *The Old Gray Mare* and *Old MacDonald Had a Farm;* then harmonize and strum to them.

## ★ Review and Suggested Assignments

1. Define the following terms and symbols:
      inversion; cadential six-four; strumming; passing tone; $I_4^6$; $I_6$; $IV_6$; $IV_4^6$; direct pedaling; chromatic lower neighbor; damper pedal; soft pedal; syncopated pedaling; sostenuto pedal; *una corda; Ped.;* *; ⌊_____⋀_____⌋; *tre corde;* fundamental position.
2. Play first inversions of I, IV, and V in every major and minor key, hands separately.
3. Play second inversions of I, IV, and V in every major and minor key, hands separately.
4. Harmonize the new songs and the earlier songs to which reference was made in Chapter VII, in every major and minor key. Review them first with the familiar usage of I, IV, and $V_7$, then experiment with the chords in other positions and patterns (you can include the V in these) and other styles of accompaniment, including strumming.
5. Play Warmup XVI in different five-finger positions which will include black keys.
6. What familiar songs not in the book could you harmonize with your present repertory of chords? Choose three and play them in class.

## ★ 8 ★

### Diatonic Scales with Standard Fingering, continued

The Group II scales start with C major and progress in dominant order through G major, D major, A major, E major. Again, these scales and their tonic minors are related by fingering. However, instead of a fixed pattern which we move in on (three middle fingers always on the three black keys, or any portion of them), we find a movable pattern which is repeated in each scale.

To determine the fingering for these scales, start with the little finger of either hand. Play 5, 4, 3, 2, 1 (down with the right hand, up with the left) to find where the thumb must come in the middle of the octave. How many fingers do you need to complete the octave? Three. So, pass the third finger over the thumb and complete the octave.

When you are ready to try two octaves, remember that your right thumb on the tonic of the descending scale has taken the place of your little finger and so must be followed by your fourth finger. The reverse of this is true for your left hand in the ascending scale.

Two observations you surely have made by now. One is that whichever scale group you are playing, the fingering pattern—once established—always consists of alternating groups of three and four: in the scale of C major the right hand plays 123 1234 123 12345 going up, while in the scale of C♯ major it will play 23 1234 123 1234 12.

Your other discovery will relate to thumbs: in the Group II scales they come together on the tonic but they do *not* come together in the middle of the octave. This is one reason these scales are more difficult than those in Group I where the thumbs strike simultaneously.

Practice the scales hands separately and *thoughtfully*. When you put the hands together, count two on each scale degree.

The Group I and Group II patterns account for two thirds of all scales. Write the scales out and mark in the fingering, but also learn the basic principles which govern the fingering so that you will not have to refer to the written score.

# Arpeggios

**Arpeggios,** or **arpeggi** (the Italian plural) consist of chord tones played successively rather than simultaneously. They are much easier to play than scales. The most important thing to remember is that the passing of the thumb under the hand or the hand over the thumb must be performed with perfect legato; no break is to be tolerated. Also, the hand, wrist, and arm must be kept level, with only a lateral or sidewise motion of the wrist. Do not try to *see* where you are putting your thumb when you pass it under.

FINGERING FOR TRIAD ARPEGGIOS
(Ascending)

|  | *Left Hand* | *Right Hand* |
|---|---|---|
| White key (major) | 5321321 | 1231235 |
| White key (minor) | 5421421 | same as above |
| C♯, c♯, E♭, f♯, A♭, a♭ | 2142142 | 2124124 |
| e♭ | 5421421 | 1231235 |
| F♯ | 5321321 | same as above |
| B♭, b♭ | 3213212 | 2312312 |

There is a difference of opinion as to the best fingering for triad arpeggios. Some pianists believe that 5321 should be used in the left hand for both major and minor triad arpeggios; others believe that 5421 should be used for both modes. Our own preference is for the fingering we have given—54 in minor, 53 in major—because, while it is true that some minor thirds have the same span as major thirds (D-F and C-E, for example), by using both third and fourth fingers each can benefit equally from the discipline of arpeggio playing. B♭ major is a trifle more pianistic for the right hand if fingered 2124, and you may do it this way if you wish, but it is easier to coordinate the two hands if the thumbs are played together.

The general rule is: if starting on a black key, put thumbs on the white key; if there is no white key, play as if all were white.

## VELOCITY STUDY FOR THE RIGHT HAND

Carl Czerny
1791–1857

## VELOCITY STUDY FOR THE LEFT HAND

Carl Czerny

## SCALE STUDY FOR THE RIGHT HAND

Henri Lemoine
1786–1854

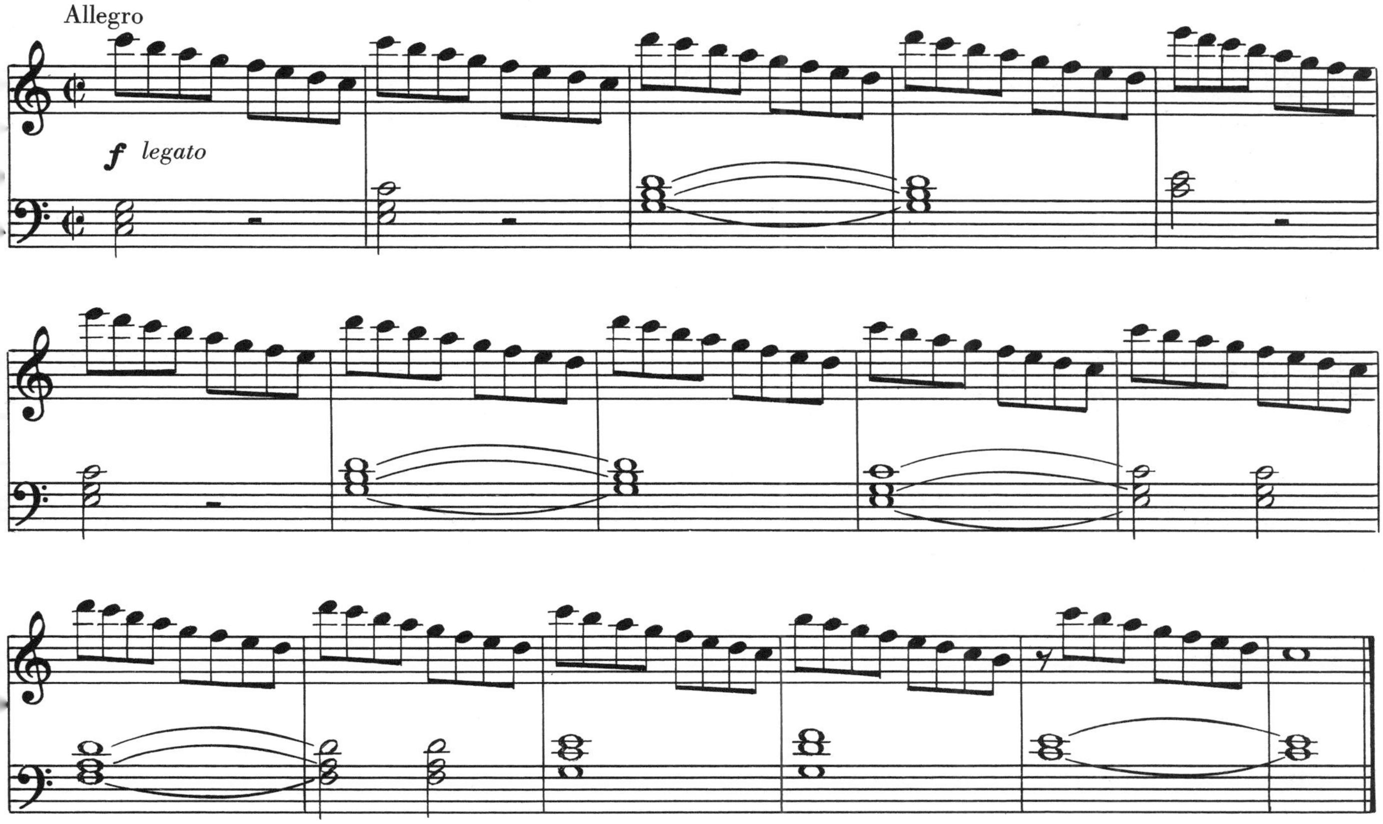

## SCALE STUDY FOR THE LEFT HAND

Henri Lemoine

Warmup XIX features the kind of thumb-under-hand and hand-over-thumb action found in arpeggios. Play it through all keys.

WARMUP XIX

Warmup XX is the reverse of Warmup I. Instead of moving *up* five scale degrees from the tonic, it moves *down* five scale degrees from the tonic. When you can play it fluently in major mode, play it in all three forms of the minor mode. Play it with the left hand also, and hands together.

## WARMUP XX

In Warmup XXI you put your second, third, and fourth fingers over the thumb as you do in scales with standard fingering. Play this in all keys, including those in which it is very awkward.

## WARMUP XXI

*Perpetual Motion* will help strengthen your fourth and fifth fingers and will also accustom you to the feeling of the augmented second between the sixth and seventh degrees of the harmonic minor scale.

## PERPETUAL MOTION

M. S. McLain

## Secondary Triads

The triads on I, IV, and V which you have been using are called **primary triads.** You can also build triads on other degrees of the scale and these are called **secondary triads.** In a major key, secondary triads will all be minor except that on the leading tone, which will be diminished (composed of two minor thirds). In a minor key there is a second diminished triad and also an augmented triad because the harmonic form of the minor is customarily used.

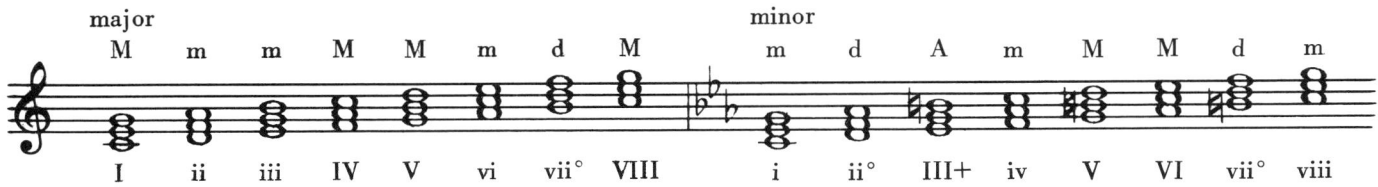

*Figure* 98.

Secondary triads are inverted and figured just as primary triads are. The four-voice chord patterns in Figures 99, 100, 101, and 102 show how secondary triads are commonly used in fundamental position. After you have played the patterns in major keys, experiment with them in all forms of the minor mode.

Figure 99 is presented with the upper voices in all three positions. In the first realization, starting with the first position, the figures are indicated. Write in the figures for the realizations starting on second and third positions. In the other three patterns only the figures are given, so write in the chords which the figures represent, realizing the upper three voices in all three positions. Be sure to write in the figures under the second and third realizations.

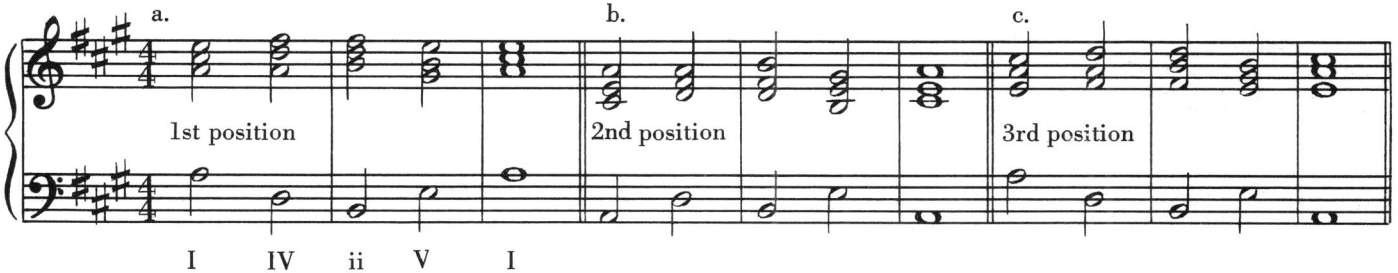

*Figure* 99.

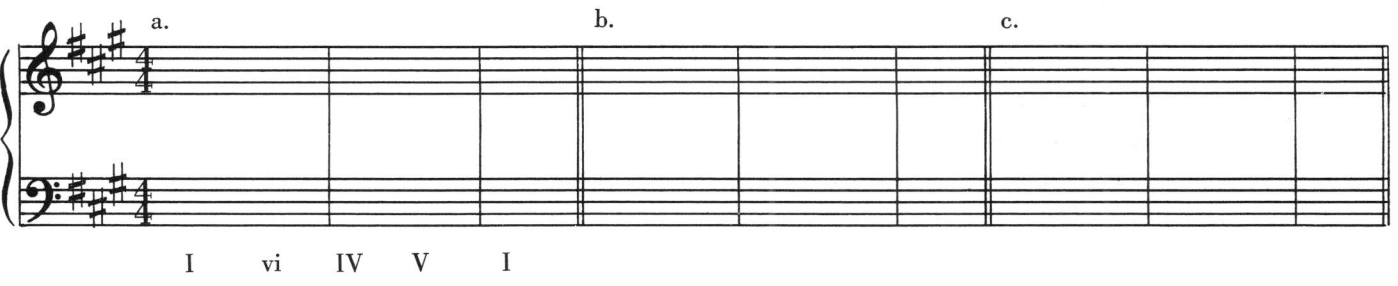

*Figure* 100.

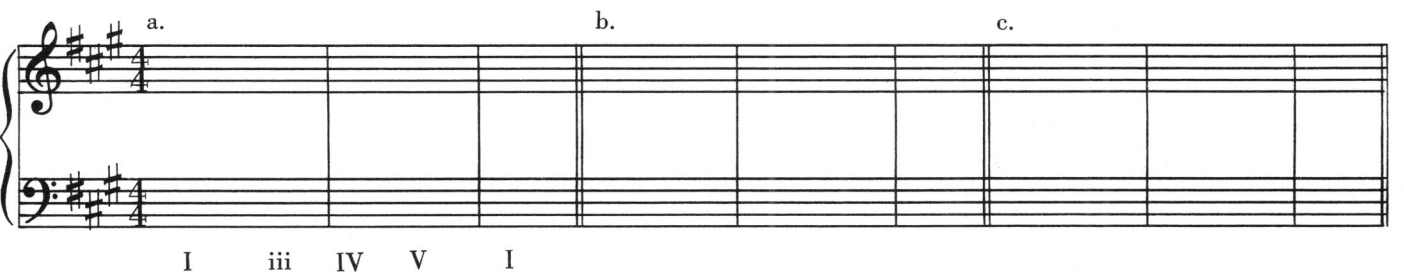

*Figure* 101.

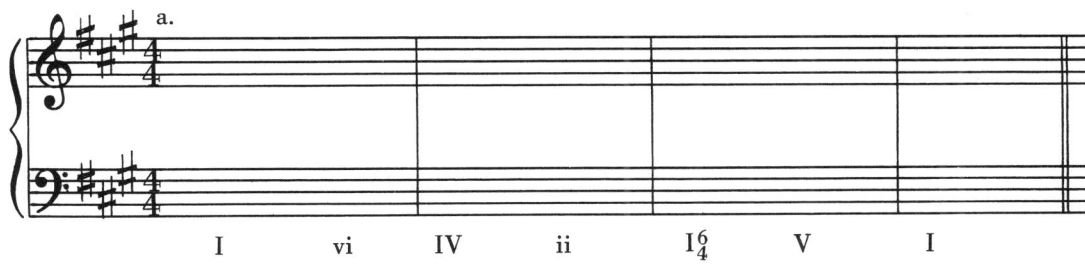

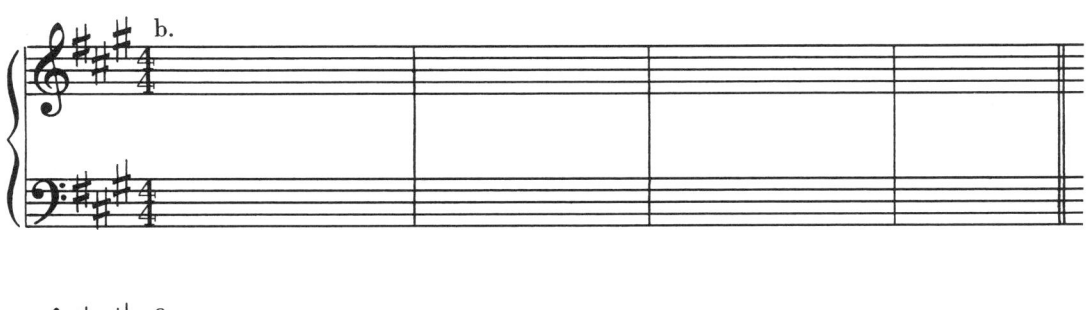

*Figure* 102.

Observe that in Figure 99 the tone which is common to the ii and V chords (B, in the key of A) is *not* kept in the same voice. In strict four-part harmony this is customary in the progression ii V which is governed by the formulation: **If there is no common tone or if the common tone is not kept in the same voice, lead the upper three voices in contrary motion to an ascending bass.** This rule will, of course, also govern the progression IV V, iii IV, and ii I$_4^6$ (no common tone) in Figures 100, 101, and 102. The rule has been observed in the examples, but there are sometimes circumstances when the melody requires that the common tone be kept, just as in other contexts it must sometimes be given up—against the rule—for the sake of the melody. Despite this one restriction, note how many ways there are in which the bass may move.

Figure 102 will be correct only when it starts from second or third position; starting from first position will result in **parallel fifths.** Parallel fifths occur when two voices in a chord are spaced a perfect fifth apart and move to another chord where they are again spaced a perfect fifth apart. Can you discover where the parallel fifths occur when Figure 102 is harmonized starting from first position? The rule against parallel fifths applies to octaves as well.

*Figure* 103.

Parallel fifths and octaves, while frequently encountered in the works of the best composers, are prohibited by the rules of strict harmony and counterpoint which evolved from early vocal writing and postulate an independent though integrated function for each voice. This does not apply to much orchestral and piano music where parts are often doubled at the octave for greater emphasis and where, indeed, formal four-part writing may have been superseded by other compositional considerations.

When you have played Figures 99, 100, 101, and 102 in block and broken chords, strum them in $\frac{2}{4}$, $\frac{3}{4}$, and $\frac{4}{4}$ time.

Ways in which the left hand alone can realize the same patterns are shown in Figures 104, 105, 106, and 107. Inversions, of course, make their appearance with this form of accompaniment.

*Figure* 104.

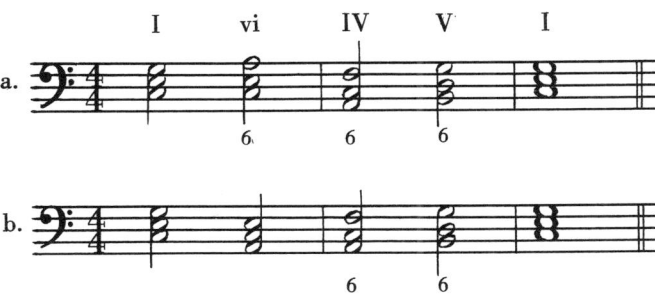

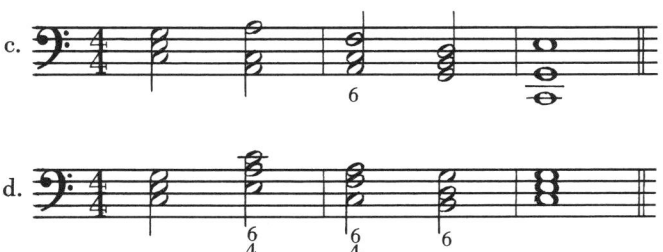

*Figure* 105.

*Figure* 106.

*Figure* 107.

One pattern which incorporates two of these secondary triads is familiar to everyone as "We Want Ice Cream," and consists of I vi ii V with the triads all in first position, or root position if played by the left hand.

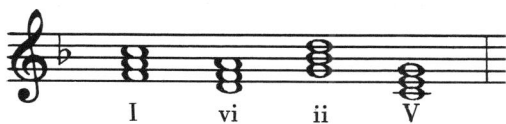

*Figure* 108.

This seems guileless enough but see what can happen when it is divided between the hands and paired with an amusing rhythm.

*Figure* 109.

Many popular songs have been based on this harmonic pattern. Can you identify any of them? Try to compose a melody of your own, to be played by the *primo* player while the *secondo* plays the accompaniment. If you wish to play both melody and accompaniment yourself, you can play the chords in their simple form (Figure 108) with your left hand. Other arrangements of this same chord sequence are shown in Figure 110.

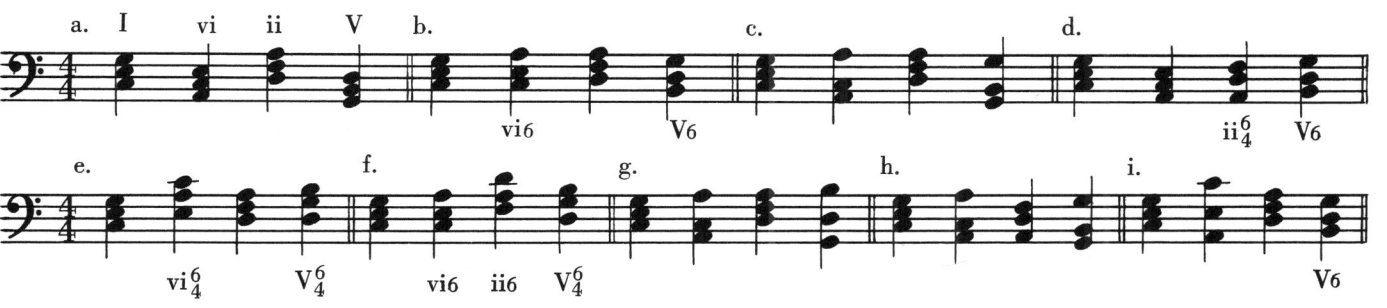

*Figure* 110.

You may ask about the "We Want Ice Cream" pattern and its flagrant use of parallel (or **consecutive**) fifths. One answer is that this little *cliché* is not very serious music but is more of a fun thing, analogous to the colloquial, slang, or baby phrases which we use but enclose in quotation marks to show that we know they are ungrammatical. Another answer is that the parallel fifths have their own melodic line and are part of the intended effect.

You may then ask: how does one know when to follow the rules and when to take off on a freer course? And, if one is to bypass the rules, why learn them in the first place? Proper enough questions, to which we answer: in formal four-part harmony exercises, follow the rules. Learning to operate within these limitations is the very best way in which to acquire skill in handling several parts simultaneously. Far from blighting any creative talent you may possess, adherence to this discipline will develop your ingenuity and resourcefulness. When you know the rules and can move skillfully within their framework, you are at liberty to break or discard them—but always from choice, not ignorance or ineptitude, and always with your good musical taste acting as mentor.

In this connection it should be understood that managing the total accompaniment with the left hand alone is quite different from dividing four voices between two hands, and requires a measure of freedom in the matter of voice leading. The limitations inherent in one hand and three (more or less) tones make certain regulations impracticable at the keyboard; for example, the rule about contrary motion when there is no common tone, or keeping the common tone in the same voice. Occasionally the rules can be observed, but they should not be allowed to cause the accompaniment to become dull and inflexible.

As guidelines in this greater freedom, the following precepts will be helpful.

1. Achieving a good bass line should always be the most important consideration.
2. Triads in root position moving in parallel motion (parallel fifths) are sometimes the best solution, particularly when they create an impression of a single contrapuntal line (as in the case of *We Want Ice Cream* and *Old French Carol*).
3. All tones of the triad need not be present. Usually the best one to omit is the fifth, but whichever tone is in the melody will often determine what to leave out of the accompaniment since it is frequently better not to double the melody tone, particularly when it is the leading tone.
4. Unless otherwise indicated, first and last chords (tonic triads) should be in root position.
5. Other chords may be in root position or any inversion unless otherwise specified.

6. Common tones need not be kept in the same voice if, by giving them up, a better melodic line can be gained for the outside voices.
7. Chords need not move to adjacent positions, nor voices to nearest chord tones, if a better melodic line can be obtained by skipping a chord tone or position.
8. If you are not keeping common tones in the same voice or are leaping over adjacent chord positions, try to lead the accompaniment in contrary motion to the melody.

Warmup XXII incorporates all positions or inversions of every triad in a major scale. Use the fingering given in Warmup XIII and play in every major key. Play it also in the three forms of every minor key. When you can play it hands separately, play it hands together.

### WARMUP XXII

## Songs to Harmonize and Transpose

Melodies may often be harmonized in more than one way. The two or more figures under some melody tones are suggestions for different harmonizations of those tones. Notes or measures which are unfigured you must work out for yourself.

### BLOW THE MAN DOWN

Sea Chanty

# WERE YOU THERE?

Spiritual

## Secondo Accompaniments

The first of these secondo accompaniments consists of components which may be combined to accompany any march-type tune such as *London Bridge*, *This Old Man*, or *Little Minka*. The three upper voices may start from any convenient position. Observe that in the treatment of the IV chord the third is introduced in the bass just as it was in the *Venerable Classic*. Can you think of other songs or melodies which could appropriately be accompanied in this way? Do not overlook melodies in $\frac{6}{8}$ time.

The second of the accompaniments is in a Spanish rhythm. Again, the components are given for you to adapt to your requirements. Construct an accompaniment to Warmup XIV b (Chapter 6), using this rhythm with appropriate harmonies. You may also play the cadences and chord patterns through all keys using this rhythm.

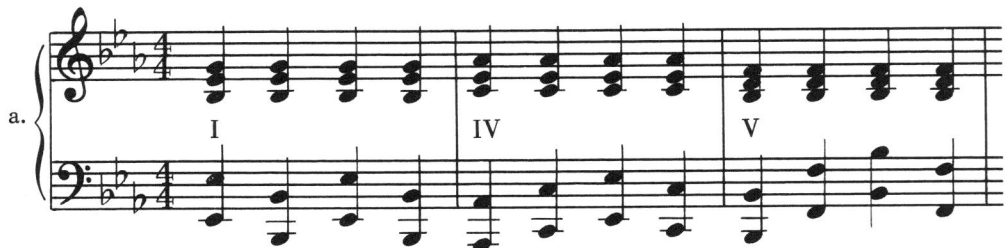

*Figure* 111.

Warmup XXIII is a double third study. The pairs of notes must be struck precisely together so that they sound as one impact. The left hand may be played one or two octaves lower. Practice hands separately first until you are sure the thirds are in unison. Play each measure four times, and play the warmup in every major and minor key.

WARMUP XXIII

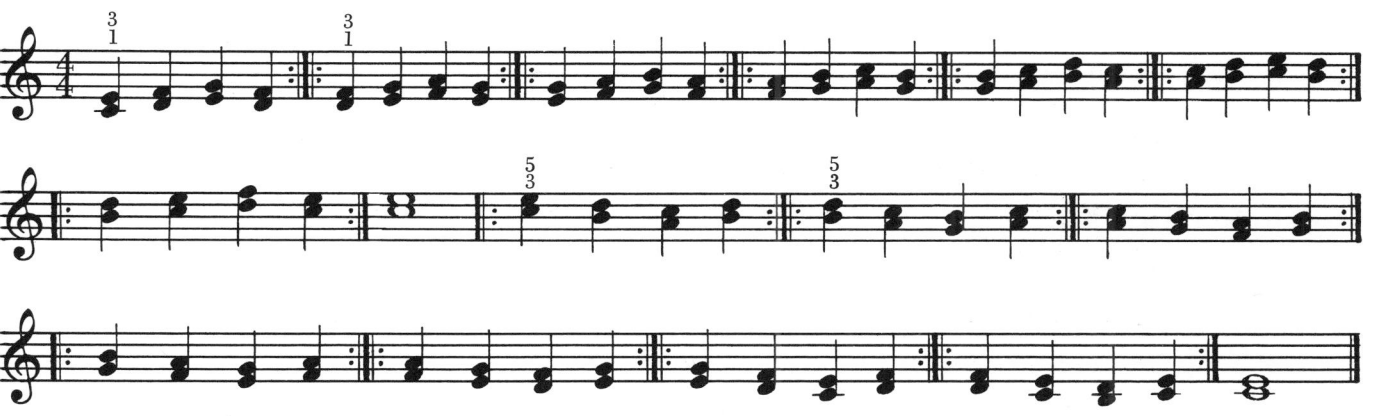

WINTER LANDSCAPE

M. S. McLain

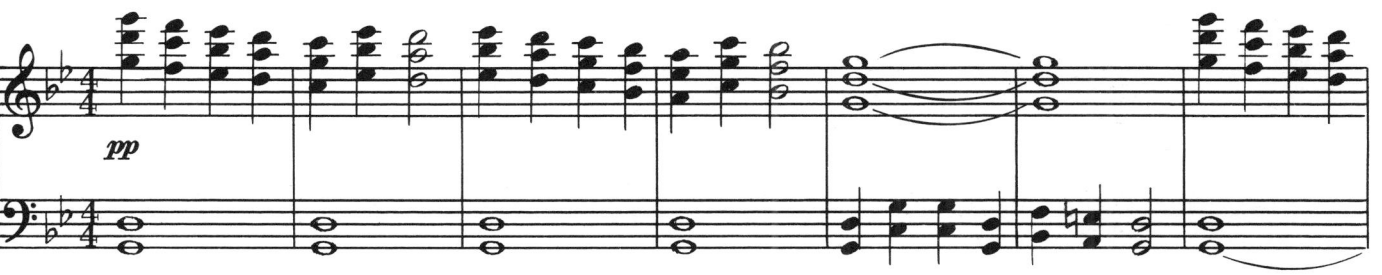

CHAPTER EIGHT 161

A tone repeated or sustained through changing harmonies to which it does not belong is called a **pedal point** or **organ point**. A pedal point may occur in any voice but is most usual in the bass and in connection with the tonic or dominant scale degrees. Two tones repeated or sustained simultaneously constitute a **double pedal point**.

A major third occurring at the end of a composition in minor mode is called a **tierce de Picardie** or **Picardy third**.

## Sight-Reading

Before playing the first sight-reading study, re-read the remarks on legato and staccato which precede *Lyric Piece No. II* in Chapter 3.

## Improvisation

You may now expand your improvisation vocabulary by including accented non-harmonic tones, inversions, and the new accompaniment patterns you learned in Chapter 7.

We shall continue to use the collective term **accented non-harmonic tone** to designate appoggiaturas, retardations, suspensions, accented upper neighbors, accented passing tones, and pedals—all of which fall on accented beats or the accented parts of beats. If you wish to do a bit of research in this area, you may, but to know the idiosyncrasies of each of these notes is not essential at this point and might create some confusion or hesitation at a time when moving forward freely and smoothly is of prime importance.

Review all of your music from the beginning and identify the accented and unaccented non-harmonic tones.

Complete the model beginnings, then work out your own improvisations.

*Figure* 112.

*Figure* 113.

*Figure* 114.

Perhaps you are now a sufficiently skillful improviser to consider a new refinement. Instead of repeating a pattern or phrase exactly, try to vary it a little. You can do this in a number of different ways. You can change the harmony, the rhythm, or the mode; you can invert one or both parts, or reverse the hands; and you can change the accompaniment pattern or modify the melodic line, or do any of these in combination—to mention a few possibilities. These are devices which a composer uses routinely but they are not too complicated for an improviser. The first two measures of Figure 114, for instance, could be varied as shown in Figure 115.

Figure 115.

# LITTLE PRELUDE IN C MAJOR

J. S. Bach

# SONATINA, OP. 36, NO. 1
(second and third movements)

Muzio Clementi

Andante

*dolce*

*la mano sinestra sempre legato*

CHAPTER EIGHT 167

# ARABESQUE

Friedrich Burgmüller
1806–1874

## BALLADE

Friedrich Burgmüller

# SMOKE RINGS

M. S. McLain

## ★ Hearsay and Other Ear Work

1. Identify the primary and secondary triads and their inversions (if any) as someone else plays the various chord sequences.
2. Play each of the chord patterns slowly, but before playing each chord (after the first) *sing* the tones of the next chord. Sing from the bass up. Do this in several keys and as close to your vocal range as possible.
3. Play by ear and harmonize the *Doxology, Vive La Compagnie,* and *Loch Lomond*.

## ★ Review and Suggested Assignments

1. Define the following terms:
    primary triads; secondary triads; diminished triad; parallel fifths; parallel octaves; consecutive fifths; pedal point; organ point; double pedal point; contrary motion; augmented triad; Picardy third.
2. On which degrees of the major scale do you find major triads? On which degrees of each form of the minor scale?
3. On which degrees of the major scale do you find minor triads? On which degrees of each form of the minor scale?
4. What kind of a triad is found on the leading tone?
5. Select and harmonize earlier songs and melodies which could be improved by the use of secondary triads in the accompaniment. Remember that you are permitted greater freedom of movement when harmonizing with three-voice chords in your left hand than when playing a formal four-voice chord progression with two hands.
6. What generally observed rules of four-part harmony are you permitted to relax in a (usually) three-part one-hand accompaniment?
7. In strict four-part harmony, what rule governs the movement of parts in the progression ii V?
8. In strict four-part harmony, what rule governs the movement of parts in the progressions IV V? ii iii? V vi? ii$_6$ I$_4^6$? ii I$_4^6$?
9. Experiment with chord progressions other than those in the text, for example: I iii vi IV V I; I V iii IV ii V I; I ii V vi IV I$_4^6$ V I. Make up similar progressions.

## ✶ 9 ✶

### Diatonic Scales with Standard Fingering, concluded

We said in Chapter 8 that two thirds of all scales fall into Group I or Group II. Let us examine the remaining third. To some extent these also fall into groups and some scales are in both groups at the same time, so these are the scales with *irregular* or *mixed* fingerings.

|  | LEFT HAND | RIGHT HAND |
|---|---|---|
| B♭ | 3214321 | Rule I |
| E♭ | │ | │ |
| A♭ | │ | │ |
| a♭ harmonic and melodic | │ | │ |
| a♭ pure | Rule I | │ |
| c♯ pure and harmonic |  | Like relative major (E), thumb on E and A |
| c♯ melodic |  | Rule I ascending, thumb on A and E descending |
| f♯ pure and harmonic |  | Like relative major (A) thumb on A and D |
| f♯ melodic |  | Thumb on A and E♯ ascending, on D and A descending |

In the melodic form of both F♯ and C♯ minors, the right hand will play the final note of the highest octave, not with the second finger but with the *third*, having skipped the second finger; but in the descending scale the second finger will be employed on the seventh degree of the scale and the thumb on the sixth, thus reverting to the proper fingering for the pure form.

*Figure* 116.

## Chromatic Scale Fingering

The chromatic scale is fingered variously depending on the requirements of the music, but for an extended passage the fingering most favored is:

| RIGHT HAND | 2 | 3 | 1 | 3 | 1 | 2 | 3 | 1 | 3 | 1 | 3 | 1 | 2 |
|---|---|---|---|---|---|---|---|---|---|---|---|---|---|
| | C | D♭ | D | E♭ | E | F | F♯ | G | A♭ | A | B♭ | B | C |
| LEFT HAND | 1 | 3 | 1 | 3 | 2 | 1 | 3 | 1 | 3 | 1 | 3 | 2 | 1 |

In this system all black keys are played by the third finger, the single white keys are played by the thumb, and the pair of white keys by 1 and 2. Except where the two white keys occur, the hands will be using identical fingers.

Practice all scales according to earlier suggestions, and in contrary motion as well as in parallel motion. The Group II scales are quite easy to play in contrary motion because the fingering is **mirrored.** (Finger pairs playing together.) There are two notes on which you may begin chromatic scales and have mirrored fingering. Can you tell which notes these are? Playing in contrary motion is more difficult when the fingering is not mirrored.

## Whole-tone Scale Fingering

Now and then one has occasion to play a whole-tone scale. As we pointed out in our discussion of pedaling, there are only two such scales, beginning on C and D♭ (or enharmonic equivalents). A whole-tone series constructed on any other note will merely be an inversion of one or the other of the basic two. Their fingering is:

| RIGHT HAND | 1 | 2 | 1 | 2 | 3 | 4 |
|---|---|---|---|---|---|---|
| | C | D | E | F♯ | G♯ | A♯ |
| LEFT HAND | 1 | 2 | 1 | 4 | 3 | 2 |
| | (3) | | | | | |

| RIGHT HAND | 2 | 3 | 1 | 2 | 3 | 1 |
|---|---|---|---|---|---|---|
| | D♭ | E♭ | F | G | A | B |
| LEFT HAND | 3 | 2 | 1 | 3 | 2 | 1 |

# Seventh Chords

Until now we have used seventh chords by rote, but it is time to take a more analytical look at them. Any triad can be made into a seventh chord by superimposing another third over the two which already form the triad. Thus the chord will have four tones, and the new tone, being a seventh away from the root, will naturally be called the **seventh.**

*Figure* 117.

Just as we can build triads on each degree of the scale, so can we build seventh chords on each degree.

Let us examine the seventh chords in the key of C major.

*Figure* 118.

Each is made up of thirds but are the thirds alike? In the seventh chord built on the tonic (the $I_7$) the lowest third, C to E, is a major third; above it is a minor third and that is topped by another major third. In other words, a sandwich: bread—ham—bread. Now let us look at the seventh chord on 2. Here we have a *minor* third first, then a major third and another minor third. Again a sandwich, but this time ham—bread—ham. The seventh on 3 is like the one on 2, but when we arrive at 4 we find a chord like that on 1. Skipping 5 for the moment, let us move on to 6 where we find another chord exactly like those on 2 and 3.

So far, we have found that the chords on 2, 3, and 6 are identical in structure, and that the chords on 1 and 4 are also identical. Now let us look back to the seventh on 5. First comes a major third, above it a minor third and on top, *another* minor third! Bread—ham—ham. (The seventh on 7, which is minor—minor—major, need not concern us at present since it so frequently is considered an extension or continuation of the dominant seventh chord—a $V_9$ with root omitted.)

So here we have two chords of identical structure — $I_7$ and $IV_7$ — which are therefore ambiguous: the seventh chord C E G B which we find on 1 in the key of C major, we can also find on 4 in the key of G major; so, without a key signature or musical context we cannot possibly say to which key it belongs. The seventh chord D F A C is even more ambiguous: it could be on 2 in the key of C major, on 3 in the key of B flat major, or on 6 in the key of F major.

Now consider our unequivocal **dominant** seventh chord: in each scale there is *only one* of its kind and it can belong to that one scale alone. Without benefit of key signature or musical context it clearly proclaims the key to which it belongs. For this reason it is the most important of the seventh chords and all the others are referred to as **secondary sevenths.** The radical difference in the nature of these two types of seventh chords is important to remember, particularly when we consider modulation.

Play the series of seventh chords in every major key. When you construct seventh chords in minor keys, experiment with all three modes.

Seventh chords can be inverted just as triads can, with this difference: having four tones they are capable of three inversions. Again, their figuring is descriptive, fixing on the *characteristic* intervals in each position.

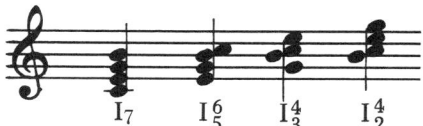

*Figure* 119.

WARNING: Be careful not to confuse *figuring* with *fingering* indications.

You will notice that the $V_7$ which you first used by rote was a $^6_5$ with the fifth (from the *root*, not the bass) omitted. The more recently introduced $V_7$ (Figures 88 and 89) was in root position, again with the fifth omitted.

**The dominant seventh.** Let us consider the dominant seventh in some of its varied aspects.

Warmups XXIV, XXV, and XXVI present it in all positions and should be played hands separately, then hands together, in all keys.

## WARMUP XXIV

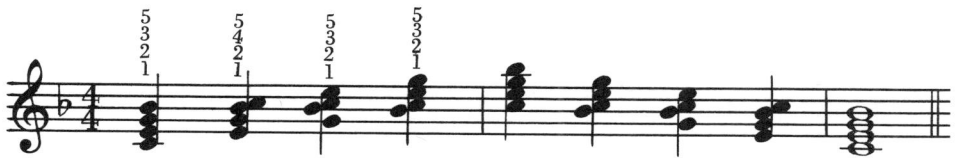

## WARMUP XXV

## WARMUP XXVI

**Three new cadence forms.**  Let us review the complete cadences which you learned in Chapter 6. You played I IV I V I with the upper voices in all three positions. This pattern presently progressed to I IV $I_4^6$ V I. Here are three more possibilities: the first is to change the V to a $V_7$.

*Figure* 120.

The second is to omit the $I_4^6$ and move from IV directly to V, always remembering that when chords have no tones in common, the upper three voices move in contrary motion to the (ascending) bass.

*Figure* 121.

The third way is again to omit the $I_4^6$ and play a $V_7$ instead of a V.

*Figure* 122.

## COMPLETE CADENCES
(in three new forms, with the upper voices in all positions)

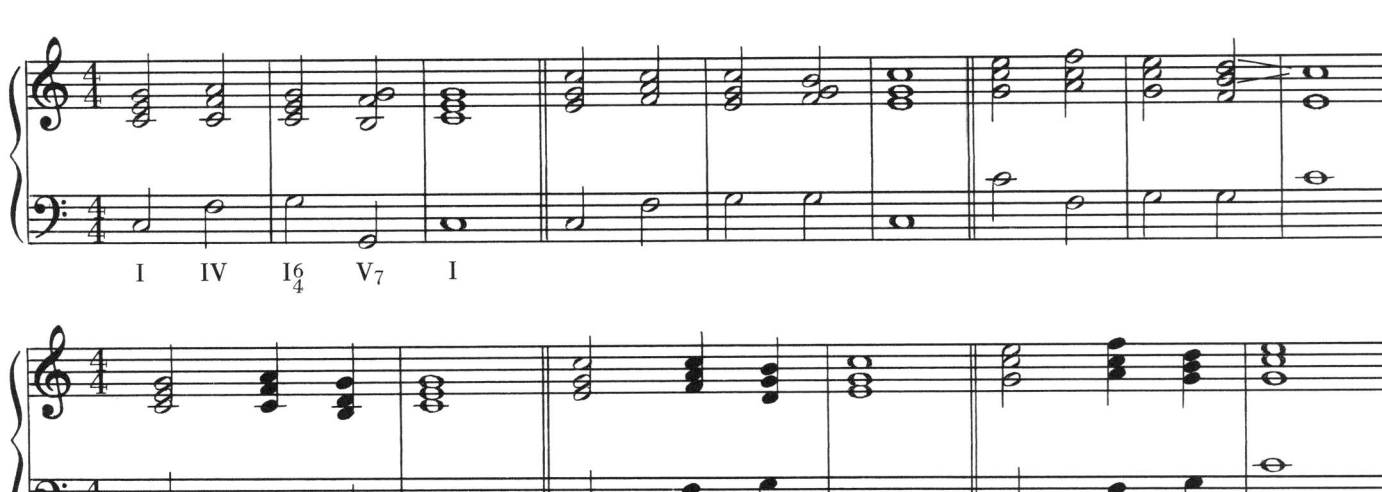

I   IV   V₇   I

*Figure* 123.

Play these cadences in all major and minor keys. You will see that the V chord and the V₇ are practically interchangeable. When to use which is determined partly by the melody note and partly by your own taste.

I V I    I V₇ I    I V I    I V₇ I    I V I    I V₇ I

*Figure* 124.

You will notice that the fifth of each of the V₇ chords has been omitted. The strong tendency of the leading tone to rise to the tonic and the subdominant to fall to the mediant has led to a formula which says that **when both I and V₇ are in root position, all chord tones may not be present in both chords.** Since the fifth is present in the I chords, the fifth in the V₇ chords has been omitted. If the fifth of the V₇ were included, the fifth of the I chord would have to be omitted.

V₇   I   V₇   I   V₇   I

*Figure* 125.

CHAPTER NINE

Play the examples in every major and minor key.

**Harmonizing with dominant sevenths.** With your new knowledge of dominant seventh chords comes a corresponding advance in the harmonization of melodies. You doubtless have learned in your harmony course that the leading tone should not be doubled. Nevertheless, up to this point, when the leading tone occurred in the melody and had to be harmonized it also had to be doubled because the only form of the accompanying $V_7$ which was available to you included the leading tone. This was the case in *Silent Night*, *Old Black Joe*, *Little Minka*, *Yankee Doodle*, and several other songs.

A few of the sight-reading studies also have doubled leading tones. This was done because you were learning to perceive a certain group of notes as a picture or symbol of one particular chord, and to have modified this in any way would have affected the picture — hand-shape — sound syndrome we were striving to establish. In the circumstances, a doubled leading tone was not too reprehensible.

Restated, the rule is that when the leading tone (in the melody) occurs on a beat or portion of a beat which must be harmonized with a V or $V_7$, omit the third of the chord and use the fifth in its place.

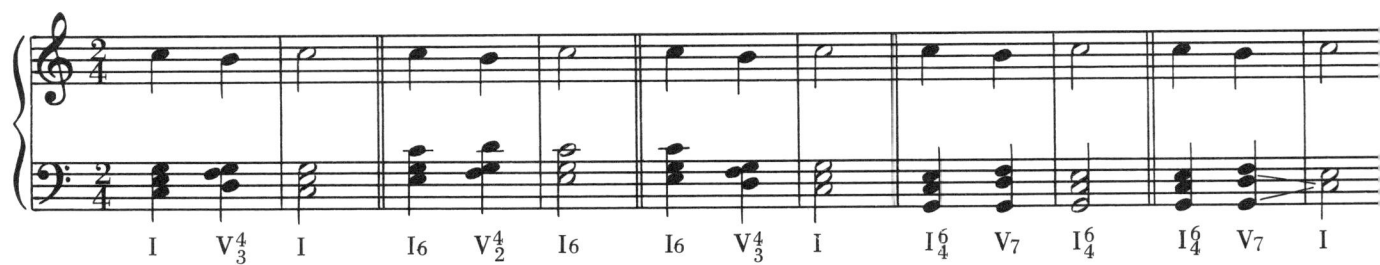

*Figure* 126.

Now go back to the beginning of the book and reharmonize all the songs which have a doubled leading tone. At the same time use, where appropriate, secondary triads, inversions, and new accompaniment forms. *Happy Birthday* illustrates the use of several of these elements as well as accented non-harmonic tones.

## HAPPY BIRTHDAY

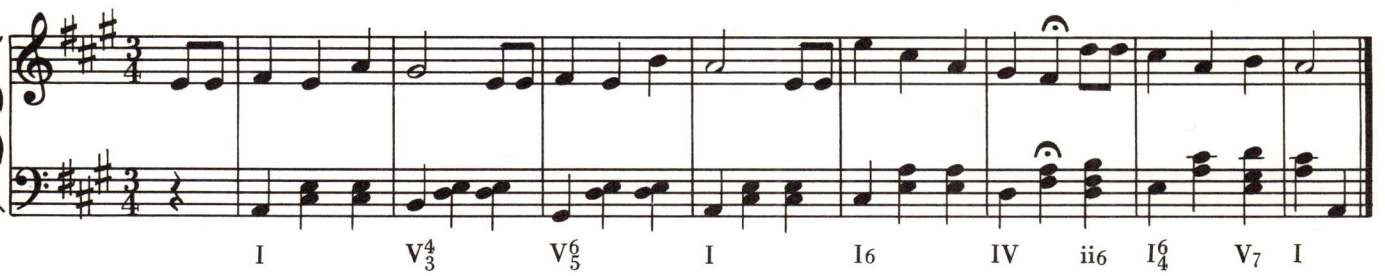

Return also to the sight-reading materials, search out instances of doubled leading tones and make suitable changes. Listen to the peculiar quality of each type of harmonization so that you will be able to distinguish between them.

When you have reviewed the earlier songs—each in several keys—harmonize the following songs, paying special attention to the leading tone.

## SKIP TO MY LOU

American Folk Song

## IN OLD MADRID

Trotere

# GO DOWN, MOSES

Spiritual

**The modulatory dominant seventh.  Modulation** means the smooth (more or less) and conclusive transition from one key to another. Some modulations are so gradual and subtle that the listener scarcely knows one has taken place. Other modulations are effected abruptly with a single chord. Sometimes one moves through several keys before reaching the objective key, and sometimes, when the starting key and the objective key are very closely related (many tones in common) *no* modulation is needed. This was the case with *Little Minka* where the melody moved from a minor key to the relative major without benefit of modulation.

As in a chess game, there are various ways of moving to one's (modulatory) objective. The one criterion common to all is that upon arriving at the objective key, the listener must have the feeling of being established in this new tonality—of having taken up musical residence there. And again, as in a chess game, guessing never succeeds; every move must be plotted in advance.

The simplest modulation, as any jazz pianist can tell you, is by means of the $V_7$ chord. Because it is unique among the chords of a given key, it immediately implies the identity of that key. All one has to do is play the $V_7$ of the objective key, resolve to the appropriate tonic, and the new key is established. This is what we did at the end of *Venerable Classic* when we modulated up one half-step. Between certain keys this is a smooth transition; between others it is crude. But it always works. The basic formula, therefore, is:

>I of the original key
>$V_7$ of the objective key
>I of the objective key

186   CLASS PIANO

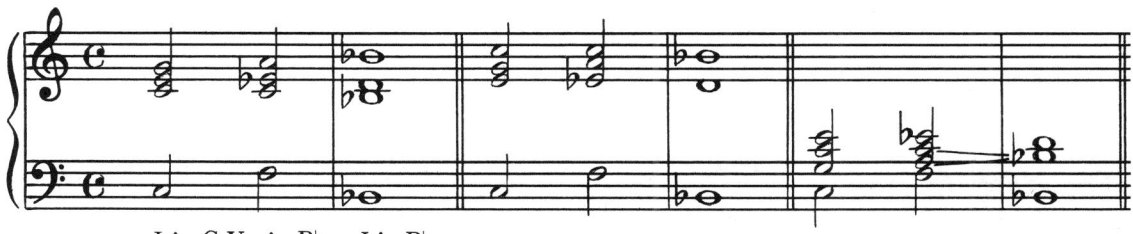
I in C  V₇ in B♭  I in B♭

*Figure* 127.

Keep the common tones (other than the bass) in the same voices, play the roots in the bass, and move the other voices to the nearest chord tones. As usual, when there are no common tones, move the three upper voices in contrary motion to the bass.

There are many times when keeping the roots in the bass is not conducive to the smoothest possible modulation but doing so for the present will help keep your thinking straight in a somewhat complex process. You will have to omit the fifth of either the $V_7$ or the final chord since, as stated earlier, all tones of each chord may not be present when both chords are in root position.

Now modulate from

C major to F major (Tonic to a key a perfect fourth higher)
C major to G major (Tonic to a key a perfect fifth higher)
C major to A major (Tonic to a key a minor third lower)
C major to D major (Tonic to a key a major second higher)
C major to B major (Tonic to a key a minor second lower)
C major to E major (Tonic to a key a major third higher)

In all but the last modulation there will be one or more tones common to the first tonic and the modulatory $V_7$.

When you have worked out the suggested modulations starting from a variety of tonics, experiment modulating from every major key to every other major key, then from minor keys to minor keys, from major to minor and from minor to major. Do this with the upper voices in all positions. Always remember that the $V_7$ is the same in both major and minor mode. When you can modulate easily with chords in fundamental position, experiment with inversions.

## WARMUP XXVII
(Modulating up half-steps via $V_7$ in major keys)

After you have played this warmup through all major keys, play it through all minor keys.

A different form of this modulation was used in *Venerable Classic*. Can you identify the difference and explain its function?

**Secondary dominant sevenths.** Dominant sevenths can be built upon scale degrees other than the dominant. Such chords are called **secondary dominant sevenths** (sometimes **neighbor dominants,** or **chromatic chords of the seventh,** or **borrowed chords**) because they do not belong to the prevailing scale, or key, but to the key a perfect fifth below the tone on which they are rooted.

For example, the chord D F♯ A C is a dominant seventh because it has the unique structure of a major triad with an added minor third (minor seventh from the root). As you learned earlier, only one such chord exists in each key and it is always on the dominant. Thus, while the root of our chord is the second degree of the C major (or minor) scale, the *chord* must belong—however fleetingly—to the scale of G major (or minor), whose tonic is five scale degrees below the chord's root. In other words, D, which is 2 in the scale of C major, is 5 in the scale of G major, and thus is the fifth of 5. If all this makes you a trifle giddy, go back to the scale of C major. Count up five scale degrees to the dominant—G. Now count up five scale degrees from the G to *its* dominant and you will find you have arrived at D, which is 2 in the key of C major.

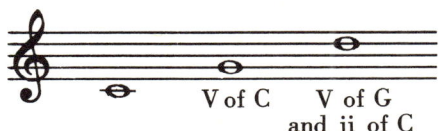

*Figure* 128.

Hence, a $V_7$ rooted on D must belong to G major, and is accordingly expressed $V_7/V$, meaning the $V_7$ of V.

A dominant seventh whose root was the first degree of the scale—C E G B♭— would belong to the key a perfect fifth lower than C, which is F major—or minor; a dominant seventh rooted on the third degree of the scale—E G♯ B D—would belong to the key a perfect fifth below E, which is A.

*Figure* 129.

The $V_7$ on 4 has been omitted because, although it is a valuable *modulatory* chord, it is impracticable as a secondary dominant seventh because the tonic to which it belongs is not a member of the prevailing key. The seventh on 5 has been omitted because it is the true and indigenous dominant seventh.

Can you find the keys to which the secondary dominant sevenths in Figure 130 belong? In the case of inversions first identify the root, then find the key a perfect fifth lower.

In case you haven't already figured out this quick way of identifying the root of an inverted seventh chord, the following hint will help: *in the interval of the second, the upper tone will be the root.* Indicate under each $V_7$ the scale degree to which it belongs.

*Figure* 130.

Although a secondary dominant seventh belongs, officially, to another key, it does not effect a modulation because it generally resolves immediately to a chord belonging to the prevailing key. The starred chord in the accompaniment to *Jingle Bells* is an example: it is a $V_7$ built on the supertonic and so is a $V_7$ of G — a $V_7/V$, but it resolves to the $V_7$ of C — the prevailing key.

### JINGLE BELLS

J. Pierpont
1822-1893

The pattern I $V_7/V$ $V_7$ I which occurred in the accompaniment to *Jingle Bells* is so frequently encountered as to be almost a *cliché*. We present it in Figure 131 with the chords in their complete form.

*Figure* 131.

Play it first with your right hand until you get the feel of it, then play it an octave lower with your left hand. At Figures 132 and 133 it is divided between the hands in slightly different ways. Which version was used in the accompaniment to *Jingle Bells?* Play these patterns as written, then strum them.

*Figure* 132.

*Figure* 133.

Since a $V_7$ is exactly the same in both major and minor modes, you may play these patterns through all major and minor keys and the only chords which will vary with the mode will be the first and last — the tonics.

The *Accompaniment to Perpetual Motion* illustrates how the $V_7/V$ is used in minor mode. Play it in all minor keys.

## ACCOMPANIMENT TO "PERPETUAL MOTION"

**Secondary dominant triads.** Major triads on 2, 3, and 6 of major keys, and on 1, 2, 3, the raised 6, and the natural 7 of minor keys may be considered **secondary dominants** and used in place of secondary dominant sevenths in some circumstances, particularly when the seventh of the chord occurs in the melody as in *Turkey in the Straw*, *Home on the Range*, and *My Bonnie Lies Over the Ocean*. (Play the last two songs by ear.)

Figure 134 shows some variations of the progression which you may use when you are accompanying a right-hand melody with your left hand. All may be adapted to the accompaniment patterns you have learned. *A* and *b* utilize the $V_7/V$. In *c* and *d* a V/V is employed.

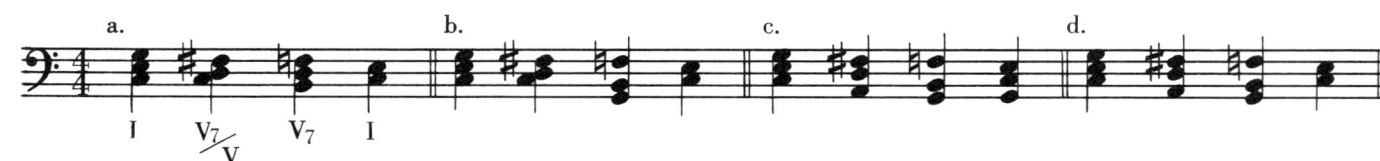

*Figure* 134.

In accompanying the songs, use a secondary dominant or secondary dominant seventh where the note is starred. Use all appropriate styles of accompaniment, including fancy strumming.

# TURKEY IN THE STRAW

*American Square Dance Tune*

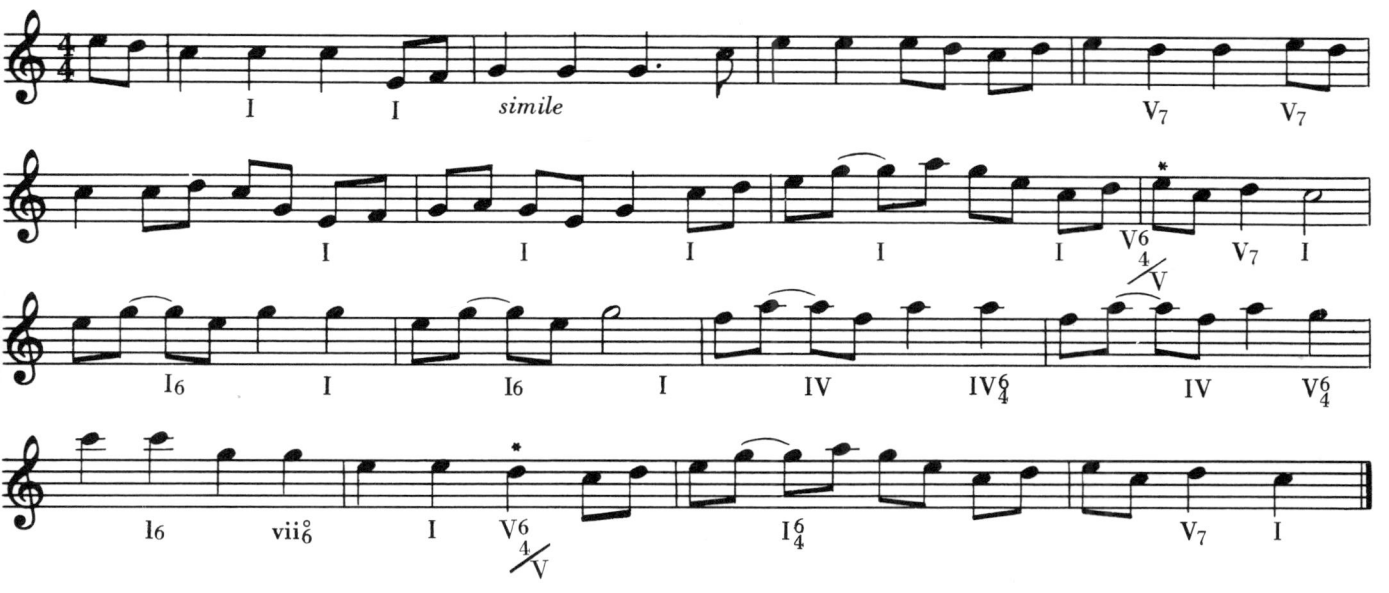

(Playing the chords on the "off" or weak beats gives a characteristic rhythmic effect to this tune. Anyone in the class who is not playing should clap on these beats.)

# DIXIE

Dan Emmett
1815–1904

CHAPTER NINE  193

(*Dixie* is another tune which can be chorded on the "off" beats.)

SHORT'NIN' BREAD

American Folksong

In strumming, when the $V_7/V$ is for only one count duration, play the hands together.

**Half cadences.** Examining the accompaniments for *Jingle Bells*, *Perpetual Motion*, and the new songs, you will notice that the combination $V_7/V$  $V_7$ occurred at the end of a section although not at the end of the composition. When a dominant harmony falls at the end of a phrase or period or section and gives the feeling of a momentary resting point in the musical journey, it is called a **half cadence.** The $V_7/V$  $V_7$ is a form of half cadence and has a strong tendency to occur at rest points in a song.

**Dominant ninths and secondary dominant ninths.** You may have wondered, as you harmonized *Turkey in the Straw* and *Short'nin' Bread*, why the $V_7/V$ was called upon to harmonize the third degree of the scale, since this tone is not part of the chord. If, however, you add another third to your seventh chord so that it becomes a **ninth** chord, you will find that your "non-affiliated" melody tone is in reality this ninth of the chord.

If you add a ninth to a true $V_7$ (on the dominant) the new tone will be the sixth degree of the scale (the upper four tones of the $V_9$ are the same as the leading tone seventh referred to on page 180); a ninth added to a $V_7/IV$ would be the second degree of the scale, and so on.

These ninths may be, and sometimes *should* be, figured as ninths — $V_9$ or $V_9/V$ or $V_9/IV$ — and incorporated into the harmony. More often the tone constituting the ninth appears as a melody tone, or as an inner voice which very likely resolves to another tone of the same chord and thus sounds more like a passing tone or appoggiatura than part of the basic harmonic structure. The following examples come toward the end of a suggested harmonization of *Swanee River*. We say "toward the end" because it is well to keep harmony simple at the beginning and save the spicier effects (secondary dominant ninths, in this case) for the latter sections or repeats.

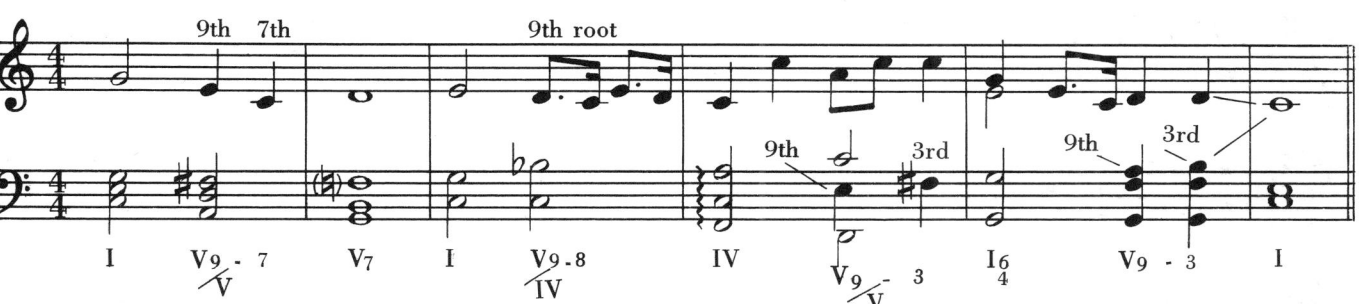

*Figure* 135.

Now go back to *Swanee River* and harmonize it, using your new chords. Can you find other songs where a secondary dominant seventh or a dominant ninth would be suitable?

**Secondary sevenths.** *Secondary sevenths* in both major and minor keys have many merits and functions but it will be enough if we consider two or three ways in which you can use them.

First, play Warmups XXIV, XXV, and XXVI using each of the secondary sevenths, including that on the leading tone, as the basic chord. This will accustom your ears to the sound of all the inversions and familiarize your hands with the shape of the chords. Do this in all major keys, and in all forms of the minor.

One very strong chord in either major or minor is the $ii_7$ in any position, followed usually by a $V_7$ or i (I).

*Figure* 136.

When you harmonize the second degree of the scale with a IV or iv chord, as in *Go Down, Moses*, this is the harmony you are using. Play this progression in all major and minor keys and in all positions and inversions.

*Figure* 137.

What are the other chords in Figure 137?

Probably the most often heard secondary seventh is the vi$^6_5$ which occurs at the end of many popular songs and arrangements. This is, of course, the first inversion (or second position) of the seventh chord on the submediant, but rather than approach it in this roundabout way, you may more easily consider it a tonic triad with a sixth added—the "added" sixth actually being the root of the seventh chord.

*Figure* 138.

The chord occurs more frequently in major mode than in minor mode, but in the melodic form, and alternating with a V$^4_3$, it constitutes the first few measures of a most famous song. Can you identify it?

All secondary seventh chords may be used in this very simple and practicable way. The *Accompaniment to Warmup XIVa* is composed of such chords and its transposition will be made far easier by thinking of the chords as triads with added sixths rather than as secondary sevenths in their first inversion. This is true also in harmonization and improvisation, since the chords are usually used to accompany melody tones which could be harmonized equally well by the triad *without* the sixth.

ACCOMPANIMENT TO WARMUP XIV*a*.

In the *Mystery Tune* we have a situation similar to that in the *Accompaniment to Warmup XIVa:* a series of secondary sevenths masquerading as triads with an added sixth. The "Tune," which you should write in — when you find it — was part of your early repertory and was harmonized with only I and V$_7$. Now, in this vastly more sophisticated arrangement, the accompaniment consists entirely of triads with added sixths. The left hand of the *secondo* maintains a double pedal point, or organ point, on the tonic and dominant, while the left hand of the *primo* carries on its own little *basso ostinato* on the fifth and sixth scale degrees — all quite independently of what goes on in the right hand of the *secondo*, or in the melody itself, for that matter.

This type of accompaniment is applicable to many melodies and imparts color and texture to an otherwise prosaic little tune.

# MYSTERY TUNE

Arr. M. S. McLai[n]

**Chromatic alterations.** Heretofore our secondary triads and sevenths have been composed of scale tones, but modifications are possible by making use of **chromatic alterations,** which means that individual tones may be sharped or flatted (as in the secondary dominants and dominant sevenths). This is done sometimes to imply a change of mode (major – minor), sometimes to aid in a modulation, sometimes to provide a color change, sometimes to secure better voice leading, and sometimes merely to humor the composer.

An augmented triad on the tonic of a major key leads smoothly to IV, taking the place of $V_7$/IV (the twelfth measure of the *Theme from Freischütz* in Chapter 7 has a good example of this). On the dominant an augmented triad leads back to the tonic, substituting for a $V_7$ (see Figure 147). Play Figure 139 in all major keys.

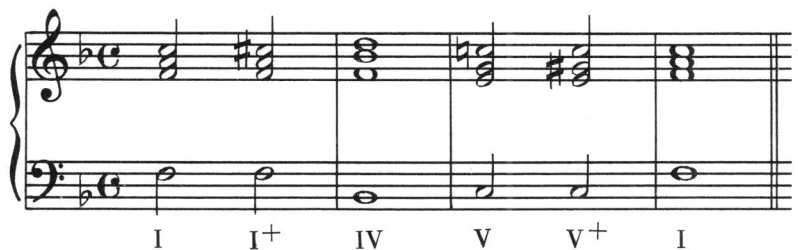

*Figure* 139.

A diminished triad on the raised tonic can lead to the $V_7$.

*Figure* 140.

Almost any diminished triad can fit agreeably into a melodic line.

*Figure* 141.

All secondary sevenths can be changed to dominant sevenths: that on the leading tone of a major key requires a change of two half steps in one voice or one half step each in two voices, but the other chords require only one voice to move only one half step. Can you discover which voice should move, and where, in each chord?

The harmonic minor also gives us that chameleon chord, the diminished seventh (on the leading tone) which so effortlessly takes on the color of other keys. Lowering any of its tones a half step converts it to a different $V_7$ and in this way can usher in a new key. Only the chord spelling needs adjusting to conform to the new tonality.

*Figure* 142.

Experiment with a number of diminished seventh chords, lowering each voice in turn, identifying the $V_7$ chord and resolving it to its appropriate tonic. Such adaptability makes the diminished seventh a valuable modulatory chord in both major and minor keys. (In the former it is, of course, a chromatically altered chord.)

Experiment also with other chromatic alterations in these chords; you will be rewarded by some interesting and beautiful effects. The *Accompaniment to Warmup XXI* features a number of such chords.

ACCOMPANIMENT TO WARMUP XXI

## Fingering for Seventh Chord Arpeggios

All forms of seventh chord arpeggios are governed by the same fingering rules. If the arpeggio starts on a white key, the ascending left hand will play 5 4 3 2 1 4 3 2 1. The ascending right hand will play 1 2 3 4 1 2 3 4 5. All fingers are used — the left hand beginning with the fifth finger, the right hand ending with the fifth finger. If the arpeggio starts on a black key, put thumbs on the first white key and play all other fingers (except 5, which is not used) in order. This applies to inversions as well as root positions.

Write out arpeggios in the various forms and mark in the correct fingering.

# Improvisation

Your vocabulary will now consist of primary and secondary triads and dominant and secondary sevenths with their inversions, all styles of accompaniment to this point, and all species of non-harmonic tones. Thus, you have many resources at your command—or perhaps not quite at your command. To deal knowingly with all these elements, together with balanced phrases, melodic lines, voice leading, and all the rest, may seem like trying to juggle twelve plates at once. To help you in this feat let us make use of chord patterns as a basis for improvisation.

To begin with, the chord patterns of any of the songs or pieces you have had can be used for improvisation. They can be used as they are or modified in any way you wish.

If you are creating your own chord patterns, it is best, for music of this relatively simple texture, to end with a tonic harmony and to introduce some form of cadence midway along. This could be a full cadence or a half cadence, and if you have learned about a **deceptive cadence** (V vi) in your harmony course, you could use that. Also, the harmony may or may not change regularly.

You will find it useful to retrace your steps by first using only block chords in the bass and chord tones in the melody, then "fleshing out" these dry bones with gradual additions—unaccented passing tones, broken chord bass, accented non-harmonic tones, and so on. Figure 143 shows such a development step by step.

## Basic Chord Pattern

$\frac{4}{4}$ I | IV I | vi$_6$ | ii V$_7$ | I | iii$^6_4$ | IV$_6$ I$^6_4$ | V$_7$ I ‖

CHAPTER NINE

Accented non-harmonic tones, and change of mode

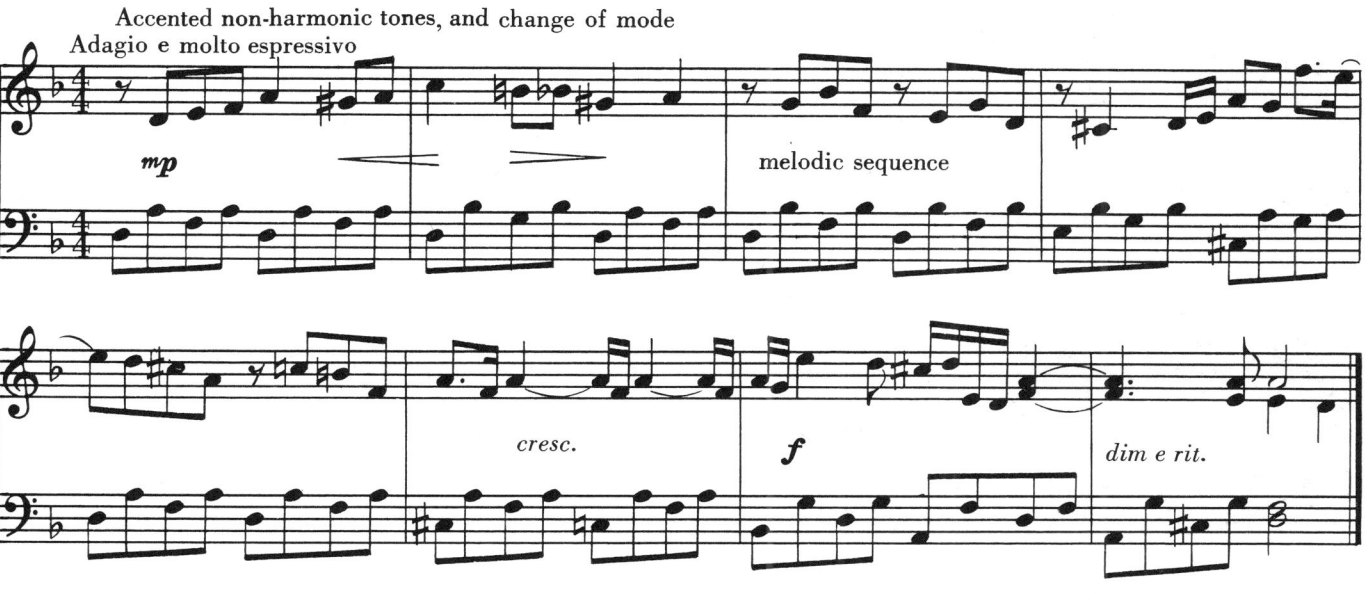

*Figure* 143.

Here are some other chord patterns with suggestions for melody note-values. Work out more patterns of your own. Use all of your present vocabulary including cadence forms. Improvise on each pattern in several versions and keys.

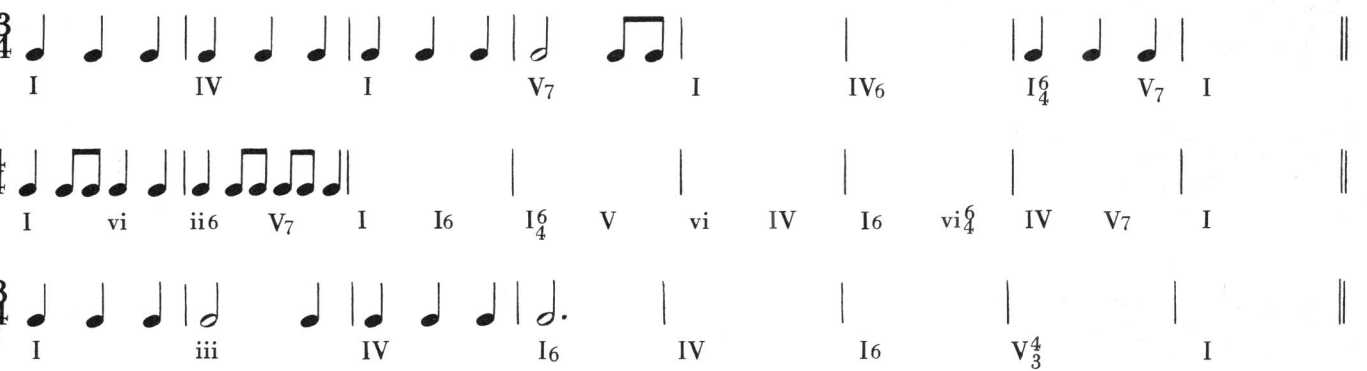

*Figure* 144.

Now try to improvise in this manner *without* a prearranged pattern. You may be permitted, of course, a second or two in which to collect your thoughts.

A useful device in improvisation is the **sequence,** which consists of the repetition of a short figure at successively higher or lower pitches. Naturally, if the figure and its accompaniment were to be repeated exactly—interval for interval—you would soon be out of the original key. This is one form of sequence but it is not recommended here. Much better is to remain within the key, merely moving the figure up or down a scale degree.

One engaging feature of the sequence is that during its course a number of rules may be broken. Among them are those relating to the leading tone, which may be doubled or led down in compliance with the pattern of the sequence.

*Figure* 145.

One rule which may *not* be ignored in a sequence is that against parallel fifths and octaves. You have probably learned in your harmony course that these are a particular threat in a scalewise sequence of first inversions. The pattern in Figure 146 provides a practically fail-proof solution to the problem. If you continue up a second octave you will see that the order of intervals in the left hand is reversed (third–sixth instead of sixth–third) so it can be adapted to almost any situation where a scalewise series of chords of the sixth is required. Play it up and down two octaves in every major and minor key.

*Figure* 146.

All improvisation is fun but here are two kinds which will afford you more than the usual amount of amusement.

The first makes use of the *Boogie Bass*. To start, try it on the tonic chord as in *Minor-Major Boogie*, then extend it to include the IV and V chords as in *Gaslight Boogie*. No one will have to tell you what to do about the melody; it can be a free-swinging, no-holds-barred happening.

The second kind of improvisation involves two players at two pianos. For this, a prearranged chord pattern is a necessity because one player strums while the other player improvises a melodic line with one or both hands. This is great fun in class when done on a rotation basis; each strummer in turn becoming "melody man" while another strummer takes over. Obviously, no stumbling or hesitation is possible here. If you find this so diverting that you can't bear to stop at the end of eight measures, repeat the entire pattern, or plan at the outset for sixteen or more measures. If two pianos are not available, two players can improvise at one piano.

In choosing your chord patterns don't overlook Figures 108 and 109 in Chapter 8. This can be prolonged almost indefinitely and finally terminated by a cadence. Decide in advance whether a plagal or authentic cadence will sound best.

A slight but agreeable variation in Figure 109 is shown in Figure 147 at the asterisk.

*Figure* 147.

The accompaniment need not always be strummed; the two *secondo* accompaniments given in Chapter 8 can be adapted to different chord patterns. Don't be afraid to introduce unaccented passing tones in the bass to achieve a smoother line than might result from chord tones alone.

THOSE BROKEN OCTAVES!

Daniel Gottlob Türk
1756–1813

## WALTZ IN B FLAT MAJOR

Franz Schubert
1797-1828

When playing a waltz bass, keep your little finger extended and rather rigid and play all the low, first beat notes with it. Do not use it on the second and third beats unless the intervals involved are too large to be played comfortably with other fingers. By keeping the fifth finger extended and saving it for the low notes, the distance which the hand must travel is minimized.

ELFIN DANCE

Edvard Grieg
1843–1907

### ⋆ Hearsay and Other Ear Work

1. Determine whether or not leading tones have been doubled as you listen to someone else harmonize a song.
2. In a random series of seventh chords played in root position, tell which are dominant sevenths and which are secondary sevenths. The series may include the leading tone seventh.
3. As seventh chords in various inversions are played, tell what the inversion of each is and how it should be figured.
4. Choose a scale in the lower register of your singing voice, play the tonic and sing the tones of the $I_7$ chord; play the supertonic and sing the $ii_7$ chord. Do the same on each degree of the scale.
5. Distinguish between the seventh chord to be found on 1 and 4, and that to be found on 2, 3, and 6. You may hum or sing the chord tones if you wish, before making a decision.
6. Play chords which your teacher will "dictate" to you from another piano. These will include dominant and secondary sevenths as well as triads.
7. "Dictate" on your piano chords for your classmates to play. Use dominant and secondary sevenths and all triads.

8. Continue to work on any of the exercises in earlier chapters which you still find difficult.
9. Devise exercises for your classmates and yourself to strengthen areas which you feel are weak. (Rhythm, chord-recognition, melodic memory, following lowest voice, identifying notes in soprano part, and so on.)
10. Play the first part of *Jingle Bells* by ear.
11. Play and harmonize *Away in a Manger*, *Cielito Lindo*, *Dark Eyes*, *My Bonnie Lies Over the Ocean*, and *Home On the Range* by ear, and in all keys.

### ★ Review and Suggested Assignments

1. Define the following terms and symbols:
    seventh chord; dominant seventh; secondary seventh; modulation; tonality; chromatic alteration; chromatic chord of the seventh; secondary dominant seventh; secondary dominant; $V_7/V$; $V_7/IV$; added sixth; borrowed chords; neighbor dominants; off beat.
2. Give correct fingering for the inversions of the seventh chords.
3. What constitutes a "close relationship" between keys?
4. Change every secondary seventh chord in a given key to a $V_7$ chord and resolve it to its appropriate tonic.
5. Which seventh chord cannot be converted to a $V_7$ by moving one voice a half step?
6. In the key of $B^\flat$ major, what is the root of a $V_7/V$, a $V_7/IV$, a $V_7/ii$?
7. How many ways can you find to convert a leading tone seventh in a minor key to a dominant seventh?
8. In Figure 148 which note is the fifth of the chord? Which note is the root? How should the chord be figured?

*Figure* 148.

In Figure 149 which note is the third of the chord? Which is the seventh? How should the chord be figured?

*Figure* 149.

9. Play all the chord progressions in Figures 98 through 102 adding a sixth to each triad. Play them in all major keys and starting from all positions. For this, each right-hand chord will have four rather than three tones.
10. Use fancy strumming to accompany *Jingle Bells*, *Turkey in the Straw*, *Home on the Range*, *Dixie*, *The Caissons*, and *Short'nin' Bread*.
11. Construct chord sequences eight measures long which include secondary sevenths, then improvise melodies to go with them.
12. Sight-read every day in a grade school song book from one of the standard music series.

# ✴ 10 ✴

## Legato Thirds and Chords

It is not difficult to play legato thirds if you have a convenient finger for each key, but what if you are required to play a passage such as is shown in Figure 150?

*Figure* 150.

True, your thumb will glide from F to G and later from G to F, but it will not be able to achieve a *perfect* legato; there will always be a slight break, and, because fingers as well as hands have a strong tendency to do similar things together, your second finger on the way up and your third finger on the way down are almost sure to break the legato line when your thumb does.

There is a way to overcome this—a way of "fooling the ear." **The thumb is lifted an instant before the second finger, ascending, and before the third finger, descending.**

*Figure* 151.

The upper voice preserves the legato and the ear is deceived and satisfied.

Lack of a finger is not the only cause of non-legato: repeated notes can *never* be legato because if there were no break between them they would not be repeated but sustained. Nevertheless, we frequently and illogically wish this reiteration to sound legato. If only one tone is involved, the pedal may be used, but if the note is one of a pair or a chord we can again "fool the ear" by connecting those tones which *can* be connected and minimizing the break between the repeated notes. Play Figure 152 through all keys, hands separately.

*Figure* 152.

When chords must be played legato, at least one pair of notes should be connected. It is best if these are in the highest voice because the ear perceives more readily what happens in the soprano than what happens in the inner voices, but if only inner voices can be connected, the effect will still be one of legato.

To play Figure 153a legato, follow the steps shown at *b*, *c*, *d*, and *e*.

*Figure* 153.

Figure 154 can be fingered in several ways. In some places you may have to use organ fingering. (Chapter 3, Figure 24.) Test various solutions, then write in the one you consider best. Use no pedal.

*Figure* 154.

The *Passacaille* or *Passacaglia* is constructed on a constantly reiterated harmonic pattern, sometimes called a **ground bass** or **ground.** This composition also illustrates the use of sequences.

PASSACAILLE from SUITE VII
(Theme and four variations)

G. F. Hand
1685–175

## Embellishments

**Embellishments, ornaments,** or **graces,** as they are sometimes called, have been the subject of much scholarly research. These little musical frills were useful at a time when ornate decoration was highly esteemed and when keyboard instruments had relatively weak tone and poor sustaining power. They constitute an almost endlessly complex study which involves the nationality as well as the period of the composer.

The subject is further complicated by the fact that composers themselves were not consistent—changing or omitting embellishments in different manuscript copies of the same composition.

Most of the old ornaments are not in general use today. This is partly because of the changed nature of our keyboard instruments and musical tastes, but even more because modern composers try to write their compositions with the utmost precision of detail and are less inclined than their predecessors to entrust the addition of notes to the discretion of performers.

Although some editors are following the practice of modern composers and, in newer editions of the old masters, are writing out the notes of embellishments instead of using symbols, a few embellishments and their symbols are still to be encountered and these you should understand.

1. The **short grace note** is written as a miniature eighth note with a diagonal line through stem and flag, ♪. In music of the Baroque and Classical periods it is played *on* the beat and given as little time as possible.

2. The **long grace note,** or **appoggiatura,** is also a miniature note struck on the beat, but it has no diagonal line cutting through it and is always of a specific time value which must be observed and which is drawn from the note which follows it.

*Figure* 155.

In music from the Romantic period to the present, all grace notes are played *before* the beat, drawing their value from the note which *precedes* them. Practically all grace notes of these periods, whether so indicated or not, are presumed to be short because notes of longer duration have been written by the composers as an integral part of the music.

3. The **mordent,** sometimes called the **pralltriller,** (particularly in German texts) is symbolized by ∿ and signifies a **principal note,** an **upper auxiliary,** and a return to the principal note.

The **inverted mordent** (or **mordent,** according to the pralltriller faction) has the same symbol with a vertical line through it: ∿; and signifies a principal note, a **lower auxiliary,** and a return to the principal note.

However confusing the terms may be, there is no ambiguity about the meaning of the symbols.

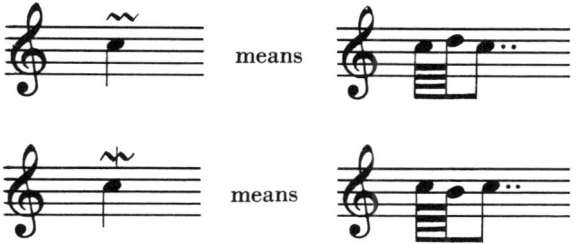

*Figure* 156.

The upper or lower auxiliaries are presumed to be normal scale degrees, but when the lower scale degree is a whole tone lower, it is sometimes raised a half step. This is indicated by an accidental below the inverted mordent sign.

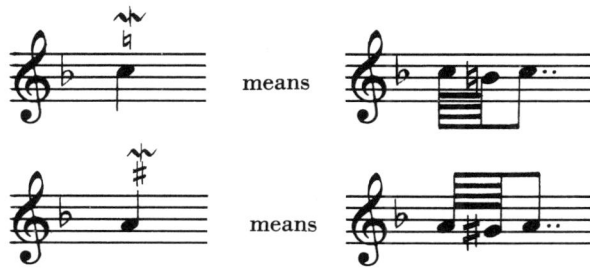

*Figure* 157.

In some unedited publications of Baroque music, no accidentals are indicated in connection with inverted mordents: if the lower auxiliary is a whole tone lower than the principal note, the performer raises it or not at his discretion.

In the Baroque and Classical periods the first note of the mordent is played on the beat, and time for the two notes is taken from that beat (as shown in Figures 156 and 157). In music of later periods the two notes of the mordent are played in advance of the beat — time for these being taken from the preceding beat. The third note (repetition of the principal tone) is played on the beat.

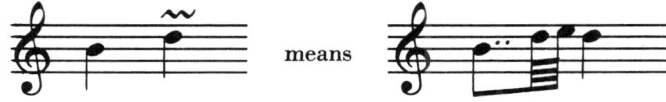

*Figure* 158.

A more modern way of writing the same thing would be:

*Figure* 159.

Tradition would have the principal note struck each time by a different finger, hence the combinations of 132, 143, 243, 231 for mordents, and 321, 213, 312, for inverted mordents.

*Figure* 160.

The purpose was to make certain that the repetition of the principal note would be heard, and not lost because of a sluggish key action or a lazy finger not releasing the key in time for it to "speak" again. With the splendid action of modern pianos and reasonable care in finger articulation, there is no need for this finger twisting, unless it results in some other advantage such as placing the hand in a more favorable position for the notes to follow.

4. The **trill** is an even alternation of two notes. As you learned earlier in Warmup XVI, this can mean any combination; but in piano music, a principal note with an upper auxiliary a half step or whole step higher is usually implied.

There is much debate as to whether the trill should start on the upper auxiliary, thereby trilling downward, or on the principal note (the one printed in the music), thereby trilling upward. Evidence would suggest that in the Baroque period at least, the custom was to start on the upper auxiliary. Moreover, it seems probable that such a trill was often *measured*—that is, expressed by a definite number of notes rather than by a rapid-as-possible alternation of two fingers on the two keys, or a *full trill*. (In a fast movement a measured trill might well represent the utmost speed of which the performer is capable.)

*Figure* 161.

Most pianists employ a full trill starting on the principal note in music of the Classical period and later, because when composers of these periods wish a trill to start on the upper auxiliary they generally indicate it by placing a grace note before the principal note.

*Figure* 162.

5. The two additional notes which are sometimes placed at the end of a trill are called an **afterbeat.**

*Figure* 163.

During the Baroque and Classical priods the custom of appending an afterbeat to a trill was so widespread that many composers did not indicate it, leaving all to the discretion of the performer.

Since even purists disagree on the precise execution of embellishments, we may remind ourselves that:

    a. In former times much latitude was allowed the performer.

    b. A measured trill is more appropriate than a full trill to a simple piece of the Baroque period.

    c. Whether to start on the upper auxiliary or include an afterbeat can often be determined by the notes which precede and follow the trill. Try always for a smooth, flowing effect.

    d. We should be consistent: do not play a measured trill one place and a full trill another place in the same composition.

6. A **gruppetto** is a group of grace notes preceding a regular note. Whether to play the initial note on the beat or in advance of the beat again depends on the period and also the style of the composition. The gruppetto in Figure 164 gives a drum-roll effect and is best played ahead of the beat so that the maximum accent will fall on the C.

*Figure* 164.

The gruppetto in Figure 165 could well be considered part of the melodic profile of the music, whatever the period, and so be played, unhurriedly, on the beat.

*Figure* 165.

7. The symbol ⸶ placed before a chord means that the chord is to be **rolled** or **arpeggiated** from the lowest tone up.

Some discussion centers around the question of whether the lowest chord note should be struck on the beat, or in advance of the beat so that the *highest* note can fall on the beat. The answer is that you must be guided by the music. If a strong accent is required, let the highest note fall on the beat. This is especially true when the arpeggiated chord is reenforcing the bass.

*Figure* 166.

On the other hand, as with the gruppetto in Figure 165, beginning the chord on the beat can, in a lyric passage, cause the individual chord tones to seem almost part of the melodic line.

*Figure* 167.

If the arpeggiation symbol spans both left-hand and right-hand chords and is unbroken, the combined notes are performed as one *continuous* harp-like chord—the right-hand notes following those of the left hand; if the symbol is broken, the lowest notes of each chord are struck simultaneously.

8. The only **turn** symbol which you are likely to encounter is ∞ although the reverse of this was also used in former times. The turn consists of a principal note, an upper auxiliary, the principle note again, a lower auxiliary, and the principal note again. The turn is performed differently in different circumstances. If the symbol stands directly *over* a note, the turn will start on the upper auxiliary and consume all of the note's time value (unless the note is of considerable duration and in a slow tempo).

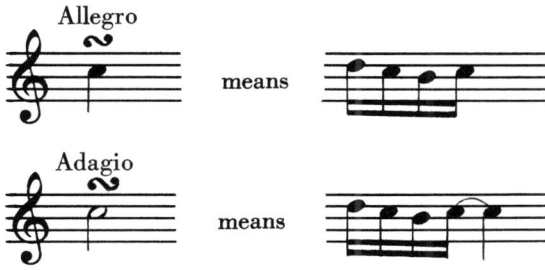

*Figure* 168.

If the symbol stands *between* two notes, the turn will consume part of the time value of the first note; exactly how much depends on the value of the first note and the tempo of the movement.

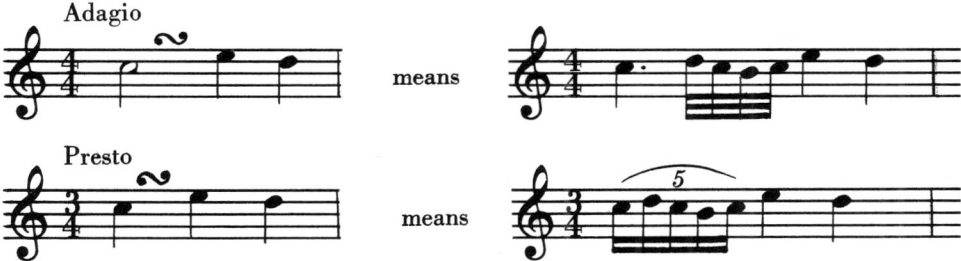

*Figure* 169.

When the turn stands between a *dotted note and its rhythmical supplement* the situation is quite different, because instead of embellishing the space between the two notes it is embellishing the space between the *first note and its dot*. The diagram in Figure 170 will make this clear.

a.

b.

c.

d.

e.

f.

*Figure* 170.

If, instead of being dotted, the first note were tied to a note of the dot's value, we would have notation as at *b*.

If we remove the tie we will have the first note, its *repetition*, and the rhythmical supplement (the final sixteenth), as at *c*.

Now let us place the turn between the first (principal) note and its repetition, using half the value of the principal note for the three notes (triplet) of the turn, as at *d*.

This is the most common way of performing the turn, but in a very slow tempo it can sometimes sound too "dragged out"; so, instead of taking half the value of the principal note we take only a quarter of its value, which will leave a dotted sixteenth for the principal note and a thirty-second to be divided between the three notes of the turn, as at *e*.

Do not confuse the dot after this sixteenth note with the original dot after the eighth note; *that* dot is still represented by the repeated principal note. There is yet another way to execute the same turn.

The only advantage to this is that in a slow or moderate tempo such distribution sometimes results in a more flowing, less "squared off" effect.

There is no hard and fast rule as to which of these three turn realizations to use when or where. The tempo of the movement will be the first determining factor. Beyond that, try to play the turn in such a way as to make it seem an integral part of the melodic line.

If the principal note is white, the best fingering is usually:

*Figure* 171.

As with the mordent, the upper and lower auxiliaries of the turn can be modified and such changes are indicated by accidentals placed over the turn symbol when the upper auxiliary is to be affected and under the symbol when the lower auxiliary is to be affected.

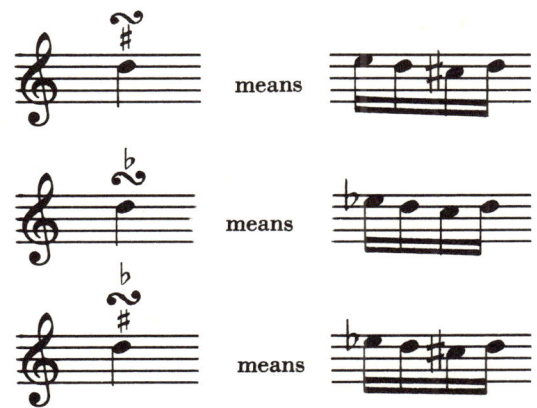

*Figure* 172.

THE TURN

Daniel Gottlob Türk

## Introductions

If you accompany a group of singers who have no conductor it becomes your responsibility to let the singers know when to begin singing and on what pitch. An introduction can satisfy both requirements.

The introduction may be as brief as one chord, with the starting pitch in the soprano if the group is singing in unison. If the group is divided into parts, the starting pitch of each part may or may not be indicated, depending on the skill of the singers. Then an upward motion of the head and a nod serve as up beat and down beat to signal the attack.

Better than the single chord system is the short phrase introduction. For this, the pianist plays a phrase or fragment — preferably from the end of the song. If the song is a familiar one, the final note need not be the same as the starting note. In *Silent Night*, for example, you could use the last four measures or even the last two. The final note is *do*, but when the singers begin to sing they will all begin on *sol*.

Look over the songs you know and decide which portions of them would make the best introductions.

## Songs to Harmonize

Two of the following songs are in minor mode. Decide which form of the minor each is in. You must also determine if there are key changes. When you work out the harmonies, experiment with secondary triads and sevenths but do not settle finally for anything which seems strained or inappropriate. When you have decided on a good harmonization, mark it in; then, play the song in all keys, using suitable accompaniments. You should also strum and use other *secondo* accompaniments while a piano mate plays the melody at the same time on another piano.

## SAINT JAMES INFIRMARY

American

## GREENSLEEVES

English Folk Song
1584?

# THE BATTLE HYMN OF THE REPUBLIC

Old Campmeeting Ai

## Playing Accompaniments

Accompanying a soloist is not the same as accompanying a group. Groups of singers tend to lag and, unless there is a conductor, you must provide leadership as well as support. This means that your beat must be strong and that you must press or crowd the tempo just a bit to counteract the slowdown of the singers. In general, you must play louder, too.

Accompanying a vocal soloist, on the contrary, demands the most sensitive *ensemble* playing. True, you give support, but you are a partner, not a leader, and you must seek to underscore and enhance the meaning of the song without drawing attention to the part you are playing.

Proper breathing is part of the vocalist's art and a good singer is careful to breathe where the very slight break will serve to punctuate the music and make it more eloquent. To have its effect, the hiatus should be observed by the pianist, too, and the very best way to achieve this unity is to *breathe with the singer* at strategic places. (Two-piano teams use this same technique for perfect timing.)

Always watch the singer. When he is ready for you to begin to play he will give you a small signal, but even after this you must watch him, because you must *sense ahead of time* what he is going to do so that you can do the same thing at the same time. Every rhythmical or dynamic nuance of the singer must be paralleled in your playing. You must *anticipate* his intention, because if you follow him you will be too late.

Of course, when the soloist has a few measures rest, *you* become the soloist. You can sometimes play at a slightly higher dynamic level and impart more character to the passage than would be appropriate to the strictly accompanying role of the music.

At no time imagine that because attention is focused on the soloist, you can afford to be lax in the musical quality of your playing. Producing good tone, shaping phrases, tapering off final notes under slurs, bringing out contrapuntal lines, balancing parts, pedaling with discretion and clarity—these deserve as much attention in an accompaniment as in a solo.

Finally, remember that a beautifully sung song creates an atmosphere—an aura—which is not immediately dispelled when the sounds fade away. To take advantage of this afterglow and prolong the audience's pleasure, the artful performer does not "let down" but holds his posture and facial expression, allowing reality to return gradually. But have you ever observed an audience, still under the enchantment of an evocative performance, abruptly and crudely aroused—the spell broken—by the accompanist's snatching his hands away from the keyboard to reach up and close the music book or perhaps to rifle through the pages in search of the next song?

Do not be guilty of such bad taste—or indeed, bad showmanship.

LULLABY

Attributed to W. A. Mozart
English translation by M. S. M.

## Improvising for Activities

Improvising for activities is one of the most rewarding as well as useful of a pianist's experiences. This type of playing can range from the primitive tomtom beat to accompany body motions of young children, to playing for "musical chairs," to producing sophisticated rhythms and harmonies for modern dance.

As a start, arrange the classroom so that there is space in which to run—preferably in a large circle. One pianist sits at a piano where he can watch the rest of the class. The class decides on an "activity" which usually turns out to be running. This may be a fast run or a moderate jogging. In either case, the class should start running in the circle to establish the rhythm and speed, and only *after* that should the pianist begin playing in the rhythm which has been established. The most important consideration is to *keep going*, and *rhythmically*. A single line of notes could suffice as a start.

*Figure* 173.

After a minute or two the pianist concludes his music with a cadence, or implied cadence, and another pianist takes over. A new activity is chosen—probably skipping—and the process is repeated.

The class will think of many activities suggested by gymnastics, games, dancing, reducing exercises, and the gaits of animals. Don't be surprised if everyone comes in next day with aching muscles and red faces.

VALSE

Grieg

# SARABANDE
(with two variations)

Handel

## ✲ Hearsay and Other Ear Work

1. As different songs in minor mode are played for you, tell which form of the minor they are in.
2. As a chord passage is played, identify augmented triads and diminished triads.
3. Distinguish between $VI_5^6$'s and $vi_5^6$'s.
4. As known diminished seventh chords are played and changed to $V_7$ chords, identify which voice moved and to what key the $V_7$ resolved.
5. Listen as a classmate plays a series of legato thirds and raise your hand if you hear either an overlapping or a break in the legato. (Each member of the class should have a turn playing.)
6. As a member of the class plays a series of legato chords, try to detect which voice or voices have the concealed breaks.
7. As a classmate plays passages (two hands) which include short grace notes, tell whether the grace notes have been played on the beat or ahead of it.

8. Repeat from a classmate's (or your teacher's) dictation melodic phrases in each of the minor forms.
9. Dictate such melodic phrases yourself.
10. Repeat from a classmate's (or your teacher's) dictation harmonic progressions which contain secondary triads and sevenths in minor keys.
11. Dictate such chord progressions yourself.
12. Play and harmonize *When Johnny Comes Marching Home* and *We Three Kings* by ear, and in all keys.
13. If you are familiar with the melodies of *I Wonder as I Wander*, *Country Gardens*, *Sorrento*, and *Waves of the Danube*, you may play and harmonize them by ear, and in all keys.

## ✶ Review and Suggested Assignments

1. Define the following terms or symbols:
   *tr*∿; ⸘; ∾; ∾; ∿; ⸫; ∾; embellishment; turn; mordent; pralltriller; inverted mordent; trill; gruppetto; short grace note; long grace note; ornament; grace; Baroque period; Classical period; Romantic period; principal note; upper auxiliary; lower auxiliary; measured trill; full trill; afterbeat; arpeggiated; rhythmical supplement; appoggiatura; passacaglia; ground; ground bass.
2. How many major triads can be constructed in the harmonic minor scale? How many minor triads? How many augmented triads? How many diminished triads?
3. Play Warmup XXII using triads in the pure, harmonic, and melodic forms of the minor.
4. Play triads in root position up and down one octave in the harmonic form of A minor. Repeat in all other minor keys.
5. Play triads in first inversion up and down one octave in the harmonic form of A minor. Repeat in all other minor keys.
6. Play triads in second inversion up and down one octave in the harmonic form of A minor. Repeat in all other minor keys.
7. In the same way, play seventh chords in root position, first inversion, second inversion, and third inversion, up and down one octave in the harmonic form of A minor. Repeat in all other minor keys.
8. Bring to class three melodies in minor mode, play them and let the class decide in which mode they are.
9. Prepare chord sequences (and write them out) containing

major, minor, augmented, and diminished triads, to be played in class for chord identification by your classmates.

10. Prepare and bring to class a series of "legato" chords. Try to play them so that your classmates cannot detect where the breaks in voices occur. This could be the same chord sequence specified under 9.
11. Play all secondary triads and seventh chords in minor keys in arpeggio form. Do this in all three forms of the minor.
12. Play mordents, inverted mordents, and turns on each degree of a scale.
13. Build a diminished seventh chord on C, convert it to four different $V_7$'s and resolve each to its appropriate tonic. Do the same on all other keys in the octave.
14. Provide introductions to songs from a hymnal, community song book, or school song book. Let the class sing as you accompany.
15. Harmonize songs in school music books.
16. Sight-read regularly from hymn books, school song books, art song collections, easy to moderately difficult teaching materials, accompaniments to instrumental music, duets, four-hand arrangements of orchestral music, and choral literature, reading the open vocal score as well as the accompaniment.

# ✳ 11 ✳

### Artificial Rhythms

Pianists are frequently required to play three equal notes **(triplets)** with one hand while playing two equal notes **(duplets)** with the other hand. As you know, a triplet is a group of *three* equal notes compressed into the time-span normally allotted to *two* notes. The triplets are written as notes of the duplet value and designated as triplets by a slur or bracket over an italicized Arabic 3.

*Figure* 174.

It is very easy to feel these groupings individually, but sometimes difficult to perform them at the same time. Such simultaneous combinations of diverse time divisions are called **artificial rhythms.** A duplet and a triplet performed at the same time is called **two-against-three.** Approached properly, it presents no problem.

The first step in the solution of any artificial rhythm is to find the lowest common denominator of the two numbers involved. In this case they are 2 and 3, so our denominator is 6. Spacing the three notes of the triplet above the six digits at every second digit and the two notes of the duplet below at every third digit will show us the exact relationship of the notes to each other.

*Figure* 175.

The combined notes result in this rhythmic pattern:

*Figure* 176.

Clap this rhythm a number of times. It is the rhythm of the *Spanish Dance* in Chapter 6 and also of the first Rhythm Drill in Chapter 6.

Now divide it between the hands and tap it on some wooden surface—a table, chair arm, or music rack of the piano—saying rhythmically, "together, right, left, right."

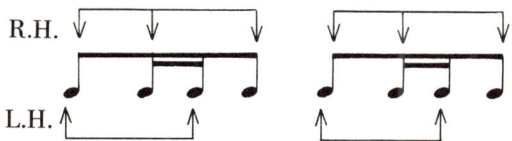

Together, right, left, right.  Together, right, left, right

*Figure* 177.

Do this for a number of measures. Reverse parts, tapping the triplets with the left hand and the duplets with the right hand, and saying, "together, left, right, left."

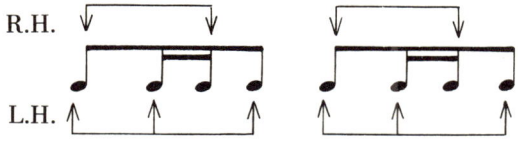

Together, left, right, left   Together, left, right, left

*Figure* 178.

When this has become easy, choose two keys on the piano—any two if you are alone, F and C if in class—and, using the second finger of each hand, perform the patterns on the keyboard, still reciting the appropriate words.

*Figure* 179.

Next, count "one, two, and three" for both patterns. Figure 180 shows how this basic counting may be adapted to three different time signatures.

*Figure* 180.

When you have mastered Figure 180, try applying the two-against-three pattern to five-finger patterns and scales.

ARIOSO

M. S. McLa[…]

There are several possible artificial rhythms, but the only other one we shall consider is **three-against-four.** We shall approach it as we did two-against-three—first the lowest common denominator, then the note-groups lined up above and below.

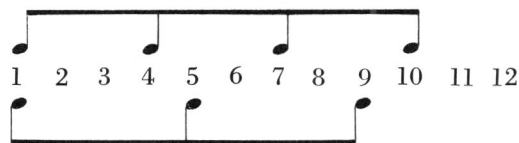

*Figure* 181.

You will notice that although the notes of each group alternate (after the first pair), they are not equidistant from one another. A mathematically exact transcript of this, based on triplets, is possible, but a bit complicated: a much easier, more practicable, and very close approximation is:

CHAPTER ELEVEN 239

*Figure* 182.

"Look! Here comes Santa Claus!" will help you remember it—or make up a sentence of your own.

Clap the rhythm a number of times, then tap it, with each hand taking turns at each part.

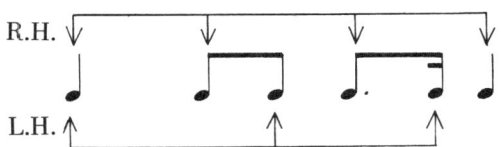 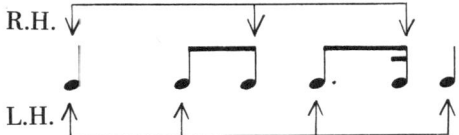

*Figure* 183.

Play the pattern on two keys, then apply to five-finger positions and scales. When the two hands have learned to coordinate and can perform at a proper speed, the slight metrical inaccuracy will disappear.

Here is a passage from the beautiful slow movement of Beethoven's *Sonata in F minor, Op. 2, No. 1*. Sometimes students avoid playing the movement because of this very section!

*Figure* 184.

One final problem sometimes arises from *consecutive* or *alternating* groups of two and three, or three and four. The well known *habañera* rhythm employs alternating groups of two and three. Several combinations are possible:

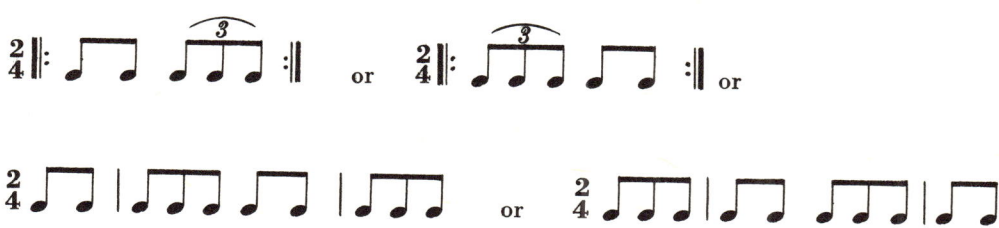

*Figure* 185.

First, clap each rhythm for several measures; then, clap one rhythm while other students clap even quarters. After several measures of this, reverse the process.

Never clap an isolated triplet: if you do you will surely be clapping ♩♩♩. The way to insure an even distribution of time is to carry the counting over to the next beat: ♩♩♩♩.

Now follow the same steps with alternating note-groups of three and four.

### HOMAGE TO MR. CZERNY

M. S. McLain

CHAPTER ELEVEN

# New Types of Accompaniment

The different kinds of accompaniments you have been using are adequate and appropriate for most of the music you will be called on to harmonize. However, you are now sufficiently advanced to consider some other styles which will add greater variety and interest to the music.

**Chords on the "off beat."** We have already mentioned this type of accompaniment in connection with *Turkey in the Straw* in Chapter 9. It is characteristic of early American plantation and country dancing, where one or more persons danced to fiddle or harmonica tunes while the non-dancers participated by clapping hands—and perhaps tapping toes—on the weak beats of the music in a primitive but strong form of syncopation. In addition to *Turkey in the Straw*, the *Arkansas Traveler* and *Chicken Reel* are just such fine old fiddle tunes which can be accompanied in this way.

CHICKEN REEL

Traditional American Fiddle Tune

**Skipbass or "bar-room."** If you have ever been fortunate enough to see, in a Western movie, a close-up of the left hand of the piano player in some *"Longhorn Saloon,"* you will have witnessed an exhibition of amazing dexterity—if somewhat dubious artistry. What this prestidigitator was doing with one hand is what you have been doing with two hands, at half the speed, and calling it "Fancy Strumming".

There is a trick to such lightning travel between low octave and higher chord. If you could see the close-up of our piano player in *very* slow motion you would observe that as soon as his hand has struck the low octave it relinquishes the octave span to which it was framed and while traveling upward in midair, assumes the shape of the chord it is about to play so that there is no time lost in searching for notes or framing the hand to the new chord. After striking the chord, the hand immediately relinquishes the chord shape and, on the downward trip while in midair, frames to the octave span. This is one of the reasons you were asked from the earliest lessons to fix the chord shapes and octave span in your hand's memory.

Practice skipbasses in various keys and with different chord patterns. Do this with exaggerated deliberation and absolutely no waste motion. Gradually work up speed, then harmonize songs for which you deem this kind of accompaniment suitable. *Little Minka*, *Lightly Row*, and *Dixie* are good choices. There are many others which you can find.

**Drone bass, or bagpipe effect.** This is such an easy accompaniment that you will have to exercise restraint to keep from using it all the time. It consists of a perfect fifth preceded by a short grace note a half step below the upper note. The grace note is so short that some pianists advocate playing all three notes *simultaneously* but immediately releasing the grace note. It takes a keen ear to detect the difference.

*Figure* 186.

Since the chord has no third it can be employed in either major or minor mode. Naturally, it should only be used where a bagpipe effect is appropriate, but remember that bagpipes are not peculiar to Scotland; they are native to Ireland, Italy, and many other lands. The two tones of the perfect fifth constitute a double pedal point and can be reiterated through various changes of harmony.

Here is another reel to harmonize in this way.

## THE IRISH WASHERWOMAN

**Drum roll.** This is almost as easy as the bagpipe effect. It consists of a gruppetto of three notes leading up scalewise to the tonic. (See **gruppetto** in the section on embellishments.) It should be played fairly low on the keyboard to simulate a deep drum.

*Figure* 187.

Do not try to *articulate* the individual notes of the gruppetto. Rather, place all fingers in position and depress the keys by means of a rolling motion toward the thumb. The *British Grenadiers* invites such an accompaniment.

## THE BRITISH GRENADIERS

**Descending scale figures.** Somewhat more complicated are descending scale figures in the lowest voice. These can be used in a strummed accompaniment as in Figure 188,

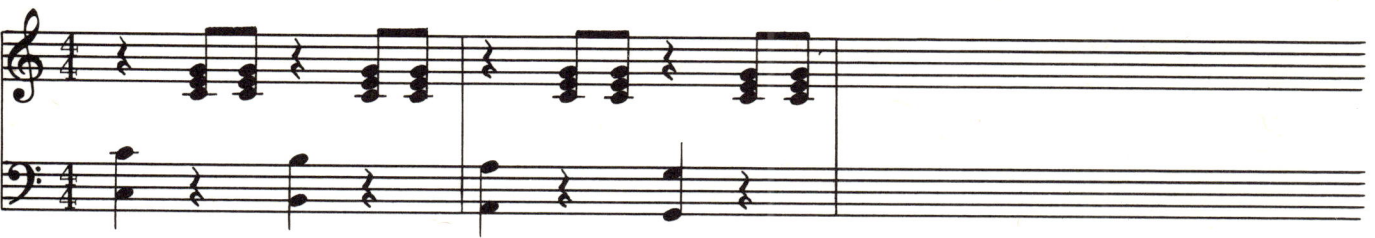

*Figure* 188.

or by the left hand alone as in this arrangement of a phrase from *The Caissons*.

*Figure* 189.

**Chords in open position.** Until now, when we used block chords in an accompaniment we usually played them with one hand while the other hand took charge of the melody.

CHAPTER ELEVEN 245

In your harmony course you have probably been working in **open position** for some time, so let us apply this approach to the harmonization of some of our melodies.

While writing in open position is no more difficult than writing in **close position,** it does seem to be a trifle harder to think chords through when you are *playing* in open position, but the richer sound of the harmonies — particularly the seventh chords — makes the effort worth while. Incidentally, most hymns are written in open position.

**Chords with more (or less) than four parts.** There is no reason why a chordal piano accompaniment should be restricted to four parts. As long as you have enough fingers you may play as many notes as you wish. There is even a way of placing your thumb across the crack between two white keys and so striking both keys at the same time, and if your thumb is long enough you can strike two black keys. (Chopin Prelude in C minor, measures 2, 4, 6, 10.)

*Figure* 190.

By the same token the harmonies may be thinned out in places to one or two strategic tones.

To serve as guidelines in such deviations here are a few hints:

1. Give special attention to outside voice lines.
2. If an inner voice is conspicuous, make sure that it moves logically.
3. Avoid "bunching" several notes in the lower register as this produces an effect of thickness.
4. If you strike a "wrong" note do not stumble and correct it, but lead it to a neighbouring "correct" note as if you had merely played a passing tone. Almost any mistake can be made to sound interesting in the texture of a piece of music if it is *quit* skillfully.

Now let us see (or hear) what adding a few notes can do for the same fragment of *Swanee River* which we used in Chapter 9 (Figure 135).

*Figure* 191.

Notice that the conspicuous inside voice is led upward toward resolution. In playing the music, bring out such a voice to heighten contrapuntal interest.

**The melody in thirds and sixths.** Some melodies seem made to be accompanied by another voice a third or sixth lower. *Silent Night* is one of these. All of it can be played in thirds or sixths with a simple broken chord accompaniment.

**Tenths in the bass.** We pointed out earlier that playing many notes concentrated in the lower register of the piano produces a thick, muddy effect, just as it does in the orchestra. One solution is to spread what would normally be a triad over the interval of a tenth. This is another version of open position.

*Figure* 192.

Even if your hand is large enough to reach the distance comfortably, arpeggiating the chord adds to its sonority. If your hand is small, swing your wrist in a wide lateral crescent and pivot on the middle note, using your third finger. Such a chord may be substituted for the tonic octave in a skip bass.

Broken tenths (the same open position triads with the fifth omitted) introduced when there is a little time to fill in are the darlings of jazz players.

*Figure* 193.

**Boogie basses.** In Chapter 10 we referred to a **ground bass** or **ground** in connection with the Handel *Passacaille*. Another name for the multiple repetition of a bass figure under a changing superstructure is **basso ostinato**. Today in so called "popular music" we have all kinds of **boogie** basses which are the logical descendants of the old grounds and *bassi ostinati*. One of these bears such a resemblance to Purcell's *A Ground* that we call it *Ground Boogie*.

GROUND BOOGIE

*Figure* 194.

This pattern requires great left-hand dexterity. Practice it slowly in several keys, then gradually work up speed. From these I, IV, and V chord components you can fashion an accompaniment to suit your needs.

Compare the basic style of *Ground Boogie* with Purcell's composition.

A GROUND

Henry Purcell
Arr. M. S. McLain

Another type of boogie bass consists of seventh chords played in broken octaves. Again we give the components, which you may rearrange as you see fit. Because the hand must be kept framed to the octaves we will call this *Frameup Boogie*.

FRAMEUP BOOGIE

*Figure* 195.

None of these various types of accompaniments needs to be maintained throughout a song or improvisation. In a very short movement it is well to take into account the value of unity, but in a longer undertaking some variety might improve the accompaniment.

There are some places where, for a brief stretch, *no* accompaniment is needed. This is so if the melody is fairly complicated or if anything in the style of a "break" occurs. For example, the seventh, eleventh, and fifteenth measures of *Shortnin' Bread* could very well be left unharmonized. In *The Arkansas Traveler* all of the next-to-the-last measure and the first beat of the last measure can be left unaccompanied, chords being restored only for the last two melody tones.

VIENNESE REFRAIN

Johann Brand
1835–1915

## LONDONDERRY AIR

Old Irish Air
from County Londonderry

## Improvisation

**Models.** All of the sight-reading studies and shorter solos may be used as models for improvisation. Analyze each to determine its characteristic feature or features.

Such features might be: notes restricted to five-finger positions; single notes in each hand; only chord tones in melody; *all* diatonic tones used in melody; chords in right hand, melody in left hand; staccato with one hand, legato with the other hand; non-harmonic tones—accented or unaccented; chromatic tones; use of sequences; variations on original melodic pattern.

When you have decided what are the characteristic features of the model, improvise (in another key but with the same number of measures and phrases) incorporating the same elements in your creation.

**New resources.** In addition to the familiar elements we have mentioned there are other resources which you have not yet drawn on in your improvisation: change of key; modulation; secondary dominants and dominant sevenths; chromatically altered chords; artificial rhythms; freer use of inversions—all of these are at your disposal, so experiment with them.

*Change of key.* Although some of your improvisation models contain brief changes of key, you have not yet changed key or modulated in your free improvisation. Now, in an eight- or sixteen-measure period, change key, then return to the original key. If the second key is closely related you may or may not use a modulation. If the second key is remote, do modulate. You need not remain in the new key long, but its tonality should be definitely established before you return to the original key.

If you plan to use a modulatory chord, figure it out in advance so that you will not hesitate or fumble when the time comes to use it.

Practice moving from all major and minor keys to closely related keys and to distant keys, with modulation and without modulation.

Avoid favorite keys in which you feel more at ease than in others.

*Secondary dominants and dominant sevenths.* Secondary dominants and dominant sevenths may sometimes be used in a repeated pattern without causing the melody to become unduly monotonous. Improvise to the pattern in Figure 196. Try it as a solo and as a duet.

$\frac{2}{4}$ I  |  $V_7/V$  |  $V_7$  |  I  '|  I  |  $V_7/V$|  $V_7$  |  I  '|
I  |  $V_7/V$  |  $V_7$  |  I  '|  IV  |  I   |  $V_7$  |  I   ‖

*Figure* 196.

You will recognize in the first three phrases the pattern of Figure 131 in Chapter 9. Create other chord patterns which include secondary dominants and dominant sevenths and improvise on them.

**Special effects.** Occasionally it is fun to experiment with what we might call *special effects*.

We have already mentioned drone bass and drum roll in our discussion of new accompaniment types, and some time ago we suggested that you improvise on the pentatonic scale.

Some other possibilities are:

a. Use of the **Byzantine scale,** which is a harmonic minor scale with a raised fourth.

*Figure* 197.

Many Russian composers have used this scale; César Cui in *Oriental* and Tchaikovsky in *March Slav* are two examples. In Chapter 4 you encountered it in *Club Zara*.

b. One hand playing black keys while the other hand plays white keys produces many amusing effects.

c. **Polytonality,** in which each hand plays in a different key.

d. Whole-tone scales. Less variety is possible with these, but veiled, atmospheric effects can be achieved by using the damper pedal to sustain the tones of either scale complex.

e. Low, spread chords, sustained by the damper pedal while you provide more movement in a higher register. If you have a sostenuto pedal, experiment with this, depressing it just *after* you have played the note or chord you wish sustained. There is also a way of depressing certain keys *silently and in advance of the playing.* Then, as you play, these prearranged tones will continue to sound while the others fade away.

f. Pedal point, the use or abuse of which can become a pernicious habit. If one does not use it as a crutch, however, it can be a valuable addition to one's resources. Especially interesting are the far-ranging chromatic improvisations which can proliferate over a dominant pedal.

g. The double pedal point, which is mandatory in what is dubiously known as "Indian Music." "Indian Music" consists (off the reservation) of a perfect fifth (usually A and E) reiterated in quarter notes in common time. These thumps are supposed to represent the beat of drums. Over them is a rugged melodic line usually based on the pentatonic scale, with an implied feeling of minor mode.

## "INDIAN MUSIC"

M. S. McLain

"Indian Music" is believed to be practically irresistable to little boys, and almost every beginners' "method" book has its entry. Since everyone else tries his hand at "Indian Music" you may as well indulge in it, too. It is rhythmical, easy to improvise, and perhaps you will think it fun. If you can free yourself from the hypnotic effect of A minor with its blank key-signature you will find that E flat minor is an ideal key for your purpose since only black keys need be used; all are available to you, and the effect is of minor mode.

One word of caution: please remember that this *genre* is a travesty on and a gross injustice to the *genuine* music of the American Indian.

**Extended periods.** In the beginning it was important for you to improvise in balanced periods of a predetermined length. Without this discipline the tendency of most improvisers is to drift along haphazardly with no idea of where they are going, and still less concept of beginning-middle-end structure. However, once you can manage an eight-measure phrase or period easily, you are capable of doing almost anything else.

Eight measures can be lengthened to sixteen by means of a half cadence at the end of the first eight-measure period, followed by a repetition with slight changes, or by a repetition in the minor (relative or tonic), or by an exact repetition with a full cadence in place of the half cadence. Then a new and contrasting section of eight-lengthened-to-sixteen measures can follow, and finally a return to the first section: an A B A form.

**Irregular phrases.** We have stressed four- and eight-measure phrases while you were gaining skill. Now you may consider the many beautiful effects to be gained from phrases of three, five, or even seven measures. A surprising number of folk songs have three-measure phrases. Some phrases have a three- and five-, or five- and three-measure, structure.

## Memorizing

Playing from memory is an obvious necessity for every artist pianist and it can be an asset to the functional pianist as well. No one will expect the functional pianist to play a Chopin *Etude*, but he may often be called upon to play Christmas carols or patriotic songs and if he knows a few of these without having to call for the music book he is in a happy situation.

If you are one of the fortunate few who can glance at a piece of music, perhaps play it through once, and remember it for ever after, we have nothing to say to you but "congratulations!" If you are like the rest of us, however, the following remarks will help.

First of all, remember that the ability to memorize improves with use and deteriorates with disuse.

Pianists memorize in several ways. Our fortunate pianist who looks at a piece of music or plays it once and thereafter knows it is said to **visualize** it. He has, in all probability, a *photographic* memory. He can, at will, evoke the image of the music and has only to play from that image. If you show evidence of this gift, develop it to the utmost. It is debatable whether or not it can be acquired if there is no natural gift.

Another means of memorizing is by **analysis,** which does not mean attaching a name to every chord, although if doing so helps you, by all means do it. Analysis in this context really means a *comparison* and *understanding* of the various elements in the composition. The way in which we analyzed sight-reading exercises No. 1 and No. 3 in Chapter 3 (page 35), or the *Four Solos* in Chapter 4, for the purpose of helping you to play them without looking at your hands, would also aid you in memorizing them. **Association** also plays a part in this way of memorizing.

Other methods advocated by some pianists are memorizing by **hand-position shapes** and **keyboard feel** (a kinesthetic approach) and by **fingering.** Some pianists memorize away from the piano while traveling on trains and planes or sitting under trees. Our own preference is for a combination of analysis and association, but you must experiment with other methods and combinations to find which suits you best.

*Under no circumstance* take the lazy way of playing the music over and over, mindlessly, until you "know it by heart": sometimes you will know it and sometimes you will not. The only thing you can depend on with this kind of "memorizing" is that it will fail you under stress.

Any kind of learning must be reinforced, so, whichever method you adopt, these suggestions will be applicable:

1. Do not memorize the beginning of a composition first. It is usually the easiest part and for this and other reasons is likely to be played more than other parts anyway. Begin by memorizing the *most difficult* part. In this way you will be reinforcing the memory impression and at the same time gaining finger mastery.

2. Divide the composition into short sections and learn each separately, then combine them into larger units. Pianists sometimes make a mistake or forget in the middle of a work and, unable to "pick themselves up" where the mistake occurred, are forced to return to the beginning. This could be avoided if the pianist, by reason of sectional memorizing, could resume playing two measures back or one measure ahead of the mishap. Moreover, the knowledge that he can do this gives the pianist an increased sense of security.

3. In all music except that in which the hands are closely interrelated, or what is in effect a single line, learning each hand's part separately can be most helpful. Such practice has the added virtue of uncovering contrapuntal values in the bass which might otherwise be overlooked.

4. It has been said that the test of really knowing a composition is to be able to play it at an excessively slow tempo. Try this.

5. If it is essential that you play a work perfectly from memory, there are two ways in which to insure security. They are toilsome but practically failure-proof. The first is to close your eyes and, away from the piano, go through every note in your mind as if you were playing it on the keyboard. The second way is to write the composition out from beginning to end from memory, and away from the piano.

One reason we have delayed a discussion of memorizing is that we wanted you to become a good sight-reader. There is no reason why one skill should militate against the other, but it is a sad fact that people who memorize readily are frequently poor sight-readers. It is not that memorizing causes them to be inept sight-readers, but that being poor sight-readers, they tend to memorize everything so that they will not have to read.

One last thought: the music is never *really yours* until you have memorized it.

# PRELUDE
(Op. 28, No. 20)

Chopin

# TWO-PART INVENTION, NO. I

Bach

# AMERICA THE BEAUTIFUL

Samuel A. Ward

### ★ Hearsay and Other Ear Work

1. Repeat longer phrases than you have done so far. See who, in the class, can retain and repeat the most.
2. Repeat short two-voice contrapuntal phrases.
3. In a four-voice chord progression repeat the bass part, the alto part, the tenor part.
4. After being told the starting tonality, identify the type of modulation being played ($V_7/V$ or $V_7/ii$) and the ultimate key.
5. As classmates modulate using inversions of $V_7$ chords, identify the inversions being used. To do this, concentrate on the movement of the bass voice. At first you should know what the original and the objective keys are, and the player should pause on the modulatory chord long enough for you to get your bearings. Later, though still knowing the keys, you should be able to identify the chord inversion when it is

played in time; still later, you should be able to identify it without prior knowledge of the keys.

6. Play and harmonize *Prayer of Thanksgiving* and *The Caissons* by ear, and in all keys.

## ⋆ Review and Suggested Assignments

1. Define:
    artificial rhythm; skip bass; triplet; duplet; two-against-three; *habañera;* drone bass; reel; open position; close position; contrapuntal device; break; polytonality.
2. Play modulations as skip or waltz basses, and as two-hand broken chords. (See Figure 85)
3. Play all seventh chords as arpeggios.
4. Play from dictation random triads on degrees of pure, harmonic, and melodic minor scales.
5. Play major and minor scales, and triad and seventh chord arpeggios in artificial rhythms. Do this in contrary as well as in parallel motion.
6. Prepare accompaniments to the songs or instrumental solos your classmates are studying in their applied course and accompany one another in class.
7. Transpose and harmonize songs in school music books.
8. Continue sight-reading as suggested in Chapter 10.

# ✣ APPENDIX ✣

### Three Little Words—Note, Key, and Tone

Properly defined, a **note** is a character in written music which indicates the pitch and duration of a sound. A **key** is a part of the piano which functions as a lever and which, when depressed, produces a sound, and a **tone** is that sound. Strict adherence to these distinctions results, however, in some ambiguities and anomalies.

For example, the word "key" means not only that piece of mechanism which sets in motion the sound-producing process, but it also means a complex of pitches which form a scale, or **tonality.** If one refers to "the key of E flat," one is more likely to mean the scale or tonality of E flat than the higher of the two black levers on the piano keyboard. Moreover, one includes in this meaning both the notes which are written and the pitches which are heard. In fact, the word "key" can refer to written pitches which are far removed, physically, from the piano keyboard, as any harmony student will affirm.

Then there is the word "tone." The seventh degree of the diatonic scale is called the **leading tone,** whether it is written, played, or heard. How odd it would seem to say "the leading note" or "the leading key." Again, when the student is admonished to "keep the common tone," he is not being restricted to what he hears, but is being directed to *write* and *play* in a certain way. Who would say "keep the common key," or "keep the common note"?

Anyone not too habituated to these terms and thereby dulled to their inconsistencies could compile an amusing list of absurdities associated with our "three little words," but one more example will suffice. Again, the word is "tone": it could (and does) reasonably connote sound, pitch, quality, intensity, duration, but how can it define the *distance between one pitch and another?* Yet, when we speak of a "whole-tone scale" to describe a scale each of whose degrees is a major second apart, we are using the word synonymously with *interval*. And when we speak of a "half tone" we might as well say a "half pitch" or a "half F."

For these reasons I have sought to use such terms as would best convey my meaning, knowing that for a musician ideas of sight, touch, and sound often are not separated but combined in one concept and packed into what Humpty Dumpty called a "portmanteau" word. Unlike children in the old precept, who were supposed to be "seen and not heard," music is to be seen, played, *and* heard, but we sometimes hear with our eyes, see with our fingers, and play with our minds.

# Scale Chart

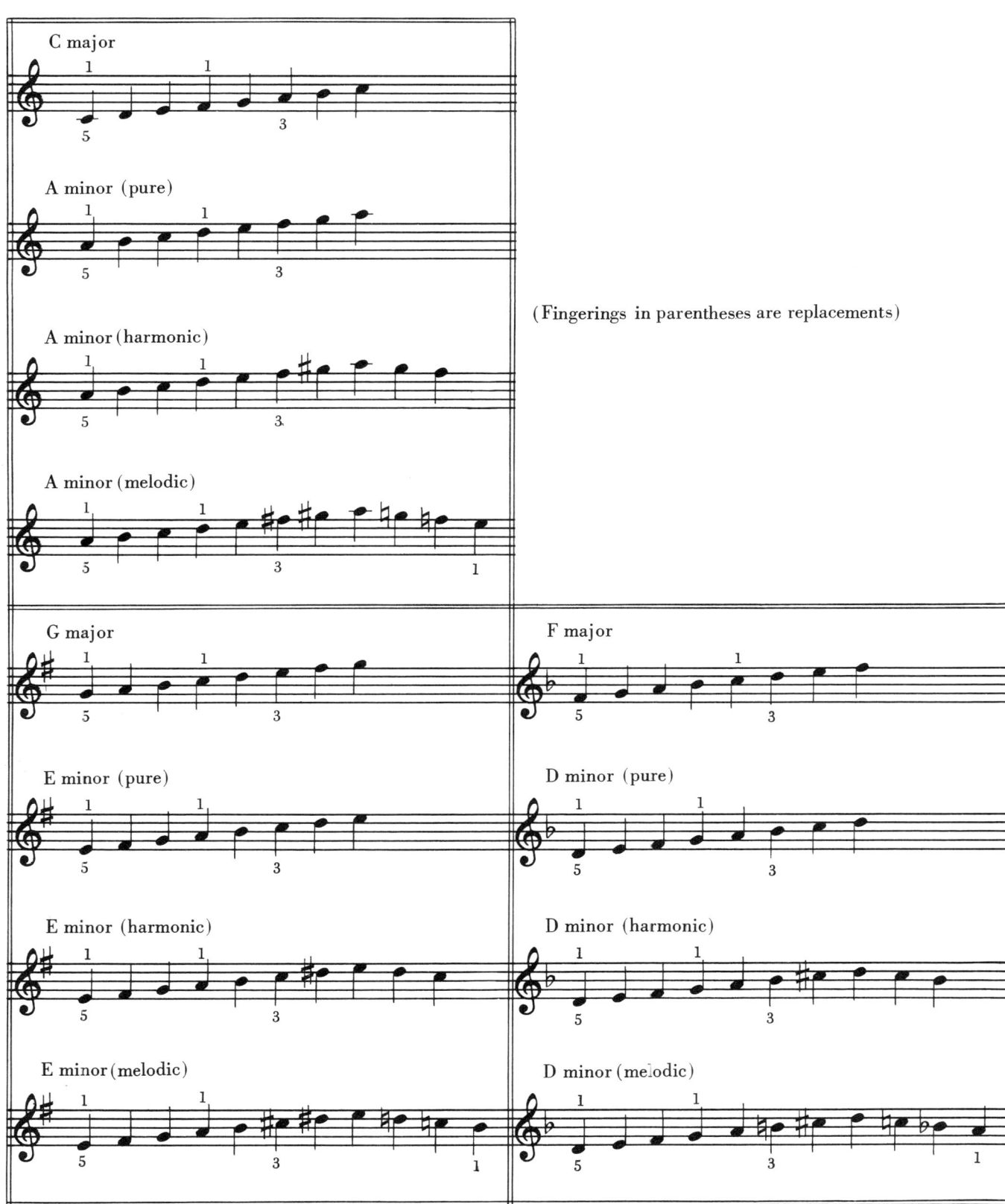

(Fingerings in parentheses are replacements)

# Songs, Melodies, and Repertory
*(in chronological order)*

## Chapter 1

Lightly Row
Oats and Beans
Merrily We Roll Along, *by ear*
Hot Cross Buns, *by ear*

## Chapter 2

Sleep, Baby, Sleep
Rosa
Theme from Finale of Ninth Symphony — Beethoven
Lyric Piece, No. I — Banberry
Jingle Bells (chorus), *by ear*

## Chapter 3

Frère Jacques
Tallis' Canon
Rousseau's Lullaby
Lavender's Blue
Oh, Susannah!
Lyric Piece, No. II — Banberry
Italian Hymn (duet) — de Giardini
This Old Man, *by ear*
London Bridge, *by ear*
Twinkle, Twinkle, Little Star *(to write)*

## Chapter 4

Theme from the Fourth Symphony — Tchaikovsky
Minor-Major Boogie — McLain
Wayfaring Stranger
Crusaders' Tune (duet)
Chorale (duet) — Bach
Song of the Volga Boatmen — arr. McLain
Pentatonia — McLain
Club Zara — McLain
Old French Carol — arr. McLain
Maypole Dance — McLain
For He's a Jolly Good Fellow, *by ear*
Pop Goes the Weasel, *by ear*

## Chapter 5

The First Noel
Theme from the New World Symphony — Dvořák
Old Black Joe
Swanee River
Minuet in A minor — Purcell
Minuet in F major — W. A. Mozart
German Dance in D major — Haydn
Minuet in G major, No. I — Bach
Circle Game — McLain
Winter, Good-bye
Old Song
Joy to the World, *by ear*
Three Blind Mice, *by ear*
Yankee Doodle, *by ear*
Silent Night, *by ear*
Auld Lang Syne, *by ear*

## Chapter 6

Did you Ever See a Lassie?
Where, O Where Has My Little Dog Gone?
The Queen's Dolour — Purcell
Bourlesq — Leopold Mozart
Little Etude No. I — Köhler
Minuet in G major No. II — Bach
Musette — Bach
Cloudy Day — Reinecke
Spanish Dance (duet) — McLain
Gaslight Boogie — McLain
Oh, Dear, What Can the Matter Be?, *by ear*
Ten Little Indians, *by ear*

## Chapter 7

Venerable Classic (duet) — arr. McLain
Clementine
Polly Wolly Doodle
Long, Long Ago
Little Minka
Reuben, Reuben
Good Night, Ladies
Theme from Freischütz
The Arkansas Traveler
Carnival — Couperin
Sonatina, Op. 36, No. 1 (first movement) — Clementi
Spinning Song — Ellmenreich
The Three Horns — McLain

*APPENDIX* 269

America (in G major) — Carey
The Star-Spangled Banner (in A flat major) — J. S. Smith
The Old Gray Mare, *by ear*
Old MacDonald, *by ear*

**Chapter 8**

Velocity Study for the Right Hand — Czerny
Velocity Study for the Left Hand — Czerny
Scale Study for the Right Hand — Lemoine
Scale Study for the Left Hand — Lemoine
Perpetual Motion — McLain
Blow the Man Down
Were You There?
Winter Landscape — McLain
Little Prelude in C major — Bach
Sonatina, Op. 36, No. 1 (2nd and 3rd movements) — Clementi
Arabesque — Burgmüller
Ballade — Burgmüller
Smoke Rings — McLain
Doxology, *by ear*
Vive la Compagnie, *by ear*
Loch Lomond, *by ear*

**Chapter 9**

Happy Birthday
Skip to My Lou
In Old Madrid
Go Down, Moses
Jingle Bells (chorus)
Accompaniment to *Perpetual Motion*
Turkey In the Straw
Dixie
Short'nin' Bread
Accompaniment to *Warmup XIVa*
Mystery Tune — arr. McLain
Accompaniment to *Warmup XXI*
Those Broken Octaves! — Türk
Waltz in B flat major — Schubert
Elfin Dance — Grieg
Jingle Bells (complete), *by ear*
Away in a Manger, *by ear*
Cielito Lindo, *by ear*
Dark Eyes, *by ear*
My Bonnie Lies Over the Ocean, *by ear*
Home on the Range, *by ear*

## Chapter 10

Passacaille from Suite VII — Handel
The Turn — Türk
Saint James Infirmary
Greensleeves
The Battle Hymn of the Republic
Lullaby (song) — Mozart
Valse — Grieg
Sarabande from Suite XI — Handel
When Johnny Comes Marching Home, *by ear*
We Three Kings, *by ear*
I Wonder as I Wander, *by ear*
Country Gardens, *by ear*
Sorrento, *by ear*
Waves of the Danube, *by ear*

## Chapter 11

Arioso — McLain
Homage to Mr. Czerny — McLain
Chicken Reel
The Irish Washerwoman
The British Grenadiers
A Ground — Purcell
Viennese Refrain
Londonderry Air
"Indian Music" — McLain
Prelude, Op. 28, No. 20 — Chopin
Two-Part Invention, No. I — Bach
America the Beautiful — S. A. Ward
Prayer of Thanksgiving, *by ear*
The Caissons, *by ear*

## Songs and Melodies to Harmonize and Transpose
*(in alphabetical order)*

|  | Chapter | Page |
|---|---|---|
| Arkansas Traveler, The | 7 | 124 |
| Auld Lang Syne, *by ear* | 5 | 78 |
| Away in a Manger, *by ear* | 9 | 210 |
|  |  |  |
| Battle Hymn of the Republic, The | 10 | 226 |
| Blow the Man Down | 8 | 159 |
| British Grenadiers, The | 11 | 244 |
|  |  |  |
| Caissons, The, *by ear* | 11 | 261 |
| Chicken Reel | 11 | 242 |
| Cielito Lindo, *by ear* | 9 | 210 |
| Clementine | 7 | 116 |
| Country Gardens, *by ear* | 10 | 234 |
|  |  |  |
| Dark Eyes, *by ear* | 9 | 210 |
| Did You Ever See a Lassie? | 6 | 92 |
| Dixie | 9 | 193 |
| Doxology, *by ear* | 8 | 176 |
|  |  |  |
| First Noel, The | 5 | 63 |
| For He's a Jolly Good Fellow, *by ear* | 4 | 59 |
| Fourth Symphony (Tchaikovsky), Theme | 4 | 40 |
| Freischütz, Theme | 7 | 123 |
| Frère Jacques | 3 | 27 |
|  |  |  |
| Go Down, Moses | 9 | 186 |
| Good Night, Ladies | 7 | 123 |
| Greensleeves | 10 | 225 |
|  |  |  |
| Home on the Range, *by ear* | 9 | 192, 210 |
| Hot Cross Buns, *by ear* | 1 | 9, 12 |
|  |  |  |
| I Wonder as I Wander, *by ear* | 10 | 234 |
| In Old Madrid | 9 | 185 |
| Irish Washerwoman | 11 | 244 |
|  |  |  |
| Jingle Bells, *by ear* | 2, 9 | 23, 210 |
| Joy to the World, *by ear* | 5 | 63, 78 |

|  | Chapter | Page |
|---|---|---|
| Lavender's Blue | 3 | 30 |
| Lightly Row | 1 | 7 |
| Little Minka | 7 | 117 |
| Loch Lomond, *by ear* | 8 | 176 |
| London Bridge, *by ear* | 3 | 28, 39 |
| Londonderry Air | 11 | 251 |
| Long, Long Ago | 7 | 116 |
| | | |
| Merrily We Roll Along, *by ear* | 1 | 9, 12 |
| My Bonnie Lies Over the Ocean, *by ear* | 9 | 192, 210 |
| | | |
| New World Symphony (Dvořák), Theme | 5 | 67 |
| Ninth Symphony (Beethoven), Theme | 2 | 18 |
| | | |
| Oats and Beans | 1 | 8 |
| Oh, Dear, What Can the Matter Be?, *by ear* | 6 | 108 |
| Oh, Susannah! | 3 | 31 |
| Old Black Joe | 5 | 68 |
| Old Gray Mare, The, *by ear* | 7 | 145 |
| Old MacDonald, *by ear* | 7 | 122, 145 |
| Old Song | 5 | 75 |
| | | |
| Polly Wolly Doodle | 7 | 116 |
| Pop Goes the Weasel, *by ear* | 4 | 59 |
| Prayer of Thanksgiving, *by ear* | 11 | 261 |
| | | |
| Reuben, Reuben | 7 | 123 |
| Rosa | 2 | 16 |
| Rousseau's Lullaby | 3 | 30 |
| | | |
| Saint James Infirmary | 10 | 225 |
| Short'nin' Bread | 9 | 194 |
| Silent Night, *by ear* | 5 | 78 |
| Skip to my Lou | 9 | 185 |
| Sleep, Baby, Sleep | 2 | 16 |
| Sorrento, *by ear* | 10 | 234 |
| Swanee River | 5 | 68 |
| | | |
| Ten Little Indians, *by ear* | 6 | 93, 108 |
| This Old Man, *by ear* | 3 | 38 |
| Three Blind Mice, *by ear* | 5 | 78 |
| Turkey in the Straw | 9 | 193 |
| Twinkle, Twinkle, Little Star, *by ear* | 3 | 39 |

|  | Chapter | Page |
|---|---|---|
| Viennese Refrain | 11 | 250 |
| Vive la Compagnie, *by ear* | 8 | 176 |
| | | |
| Waves of the Danube, *by ear* | 10 | 234 |
| Wayfaring Stranger | 4 | 44 |
| We Three Kings, *by ear* | 10 | 234 |
| Were You There? | 8 | 160 |
| When Johnny Comes Marching Home, *by ear* | 10 | 234 |
| Where, O Where Has My Little Dog Gone? | 6 | 93 |
| Winter, Good-bye | 5 | 75 |
| | | |
| Yankee Doodle, *by ear* | 5 | 78 |

# Repertory
*(in alphabetical order)*

|  | Chapter | Page |
|---|---|---|
| Accompaniment to *Perpetual Motion* | 9 | 192 |
| Accompaniment to *Warmup XIVa* | 9 | 197 |
| Accompaniment to *Warmup XXI* | 9 | 200 |
| America, in G major — Carey | 7 | 143 |
| America the Beautiful — S. A. Ward | 11 | 260 |
| Arabesque — Burgmüller | 8 | 170 |
| Arioso — McLain | 11 | 238 |
| | | |
| Ballade — Burgmüller | 8 | 171 |
| Bourlesq — L. Mozart | 6 | 97 |
| | | |
| Carnival — Couperin | 7 | 137 |
| Chorale (four hands) — Bach | 4 | 49 |
| Circle Game — McLain | 5 | 74 |
| Cloudy Day — Reinecke | 6 | 102 |
| Club Zara — McLain | 4 | 55 |
| Crusaders' Tune (four hands) | 4 | 47 |
| | | |
| Elfin Dance — Grieg | 9 | 207 |
| | | |
| Gaslight Boogie — McLain | 6 | 104 |
| German Dance in D major — Haydn | 5 | 72 |
| Ground, A — Purcell | 11 | 248 |
| | | |
| Happy Birthday | 9 | 185 |
| Homage to Mr. Czerny — McLain | 11 | 241 |
| | | |
| "Indian Music" — McLain | 11 | 254 |
| Italian Hymn (four hands) — de Giardini | 3 | 33 |
| | | |
| Jingle Bells — J. Pierpont | 9 | 190 |
| | | |
| Little Etude No. I — Köhler | 6 | 98 |
| Little Prelude in C major — Bach | 8 | 166 |
| Lullaby (song) — W. A. Mozart | 10 | 227 |
| Lyric Piece No. I — Banberry | 2 | 19 |
| Lyric Piece No. II — Banberry | 3 | 32 |

|  | Chapter | Page |
|---|---|---|
| Maypole Dance — McLain | 4 | 56 |
| Menuet in F major — W. A. Mozart | 5 | 72 |
| Minor-Major Boogie — McLain | 4 | 41 |
| Minuet in A minor — Purcell | 5 | 71 |
| Minuet in G major No. I — Bach | 5 | 73 |
| Minuet in G major No. II — Bach | 6 | 99 |
| Musette — Bach | 6 | 100 |
| Mystery Tune (four hands) — McLain | 9 | 198 |
| Ninth Symphony, Theme — Beethoven | 2 | 18 |
| Old French Carol — arr. McLain | 4 | 55 |
| Passacaille — Handel | 10 | 214 |
| Pentatonia — McLain | 4 | 54 |
| Perpetual Motion — McLain | 8 | 151 |
| Prelude, Op. 28, No. 20 — Chopin | 11 | 257 |
| Queen's Dolour, The — Purcell | 6 | 97 |
| Sarabande — Handel | 10 | 232 |
| Scale Study for the Left Hand — Lemoine | 8 | 149 |
| Scale Study for the Right Hand — Lemoine | 8 | 149 |
| Smoke Rings — McLain | 8 | 174 |
| Sonatina, Op. 36, No. I (first movement) — Clementi | 7 | 138 |
| Sonatina, Op. 36, No. I (second and third movements) — Clementi | 8 | 166 |
| Song of the Volga Boatmen — arr. McLain | 4 | 50 |
| Spanish Dance (four hands) — McLain | 6 | 102 |
| Spinning Song — Ellmenreich | 7 | 140 |
| Star-Spangled Banner, in A flat major, The — J. S. Smith | 7 | 143 |
| Tallis' Canon — Tallis | 3 | 28 |
| Those Broken Octaves! — Türk | 9 | 205 |
| Three Horns, The — McLain | 7 | 142 |
| Turn, The — Türk | 10 | 223 |
| Two-Part Invention, No. I — Bach | 11 | 258 |
| Valse — Grieg | 10 | 229 |
| Velocity Study for the Left Hand — Czerny | 8 | 148 |
| Velocity Study for the Right Hand — Czerny | 8 | 148 |
| Venerable Classic (four hands) | 7 | 112 |
| Waltz in B flat major — Schubert | 9 | 206 |
| Winter Landscape — McLain | 8 | 161 |

# Index

Accompaniment patterns, 92, 115, 118 (*see also* Accompaniments)
Accompaniments:
    alternating root and fifth, 114, 117
    bagpipe effect, 243
    "bar-room," 242
    *basso ostinato*, 197, 248
    block chord, 92, 117, 155
    boogie bass, 41, 59, 104, 204, 248
    broken chord, 92, 155
    chords in open position, 245
    chords with other than four parts, 155–159, 192, 246
    descending scale figures, 245
    drone bass, 243
    drum roll, 244
    "Frameup Boogie," 249
    ground bass, 214, 248
    "Ground Boogie," 248
    left-hand, 117, 155–159, 192
    left-hand chord progressions, 155–159, 192 (*see also* Chord patterns)
    melody in thirds and sixths, 247
    new types, 242
    off-beat, 193, 242
    playing, 226
    *secondo*, 160
    skipbass, 242
    strumming, 114, 204
    tenths in bass, 247
    waltz bass, 207
Added sixth, 196 (*see also* Chords: $vi^6_5$)
Arpeggios, 147
    fingering for (*see* Fingering)
    seventh chord, 200
    triad, 147

Bass, 84, 114–115, 117, 256
    boogie (*see* Accompaniments)
    figured, 28, 152
    ground, 248
    part, 260 (*see also* Voice)
    in tenths, 247
    waltz, 207
*Basso ostinato* (*see* Accompaniments)
Beat:
    down, 224
    up, 224
Bell-ringing, 63

Block chords (*see* Chords)
Boogie bass (*see* Accompaniments)
"Break," 250
Breaking rules, 158
Broken chords, 92 (*see also* Chords)

Cadence:
    authentic, 87, 120
    church, 87
    complete, 87, 120, 182
    deceptive, 201
    defined, 87
    forms, 87–88, 120, 122, 181–183, 194, 201, 254
    half, 194, 254
    plagal, 87
Cadential six-four, 120 (*see also* Chords)
Canon, 27
Changes, 63
Chord patterns: (*see also* Accompaniments)
    for improvisation, 201, 203, 252 (*see also* Improvisation)
    left-hand, 144, 173 (*see also* Accompaniments)
    with secondary dominants, 190, 192, 252
    with secondary triads, 152, 154, 201, 203
    for sequence of sixths, 204
Chord progressions (*see* Chord patterns)
Chords:
    arpeggiated, 220 (*see* Embellishments)
    block, 92, 117, 155
    broken, 92, 155
    cadential six-four, 120
    dominant ninth, 180, 194
    $V_7$ (*see* Chords, seventh, dominant)
    $IV_6$, 122
    in open position, 245
    with other than four parts, 246
    seventh, 179
        diminished, modulating by means of, 199
        dominant, 15, 122, 179–180
        dominant, harmonizing with, 184
        dominant, modulating by means of, 124, 186
        dominant, in root position, 122
        inverted, 180 (*see also* Inversions)
        locating root of, 189
        secondary, 180, 195
        secondary dominant, 188, 252
        $vi^6_5$, 196
        $ii_7$, or $II_7$, 195
    triads, 14
        augmented, 152
        diminished, 152
        dominant, 86
        inverted (*see* Inversions)
        locating root of, 84
        major, 14, 40, 82
        minor, 40, 82, 152
        position of major and minor thirds in, 141
        secondary, 152
        secondary dominant, 192, 252

Chords (continued)
    triads (continued)
        subdominant, 30
        subdominant in minor mode, 43
        tonic, 14
Chordwise, 17
Chromatic alterations, 198
Chromatic lower neighbor (*see* Non-harmonic tones)
Chromatic order, 64
Chromatic scale (*see* Scale fingering and Scale structure)
Circle of fifths, 65
Circle of fourths, 65
Circle of keys, 64
Clusters, note, 34, 110
Common tone:
    defined, 85
    rule for giving up, 154
    rule for keeping, 85
Consecutive fifths (*see* Parallel fifths)
Counting aloud, 5
Covered hands, 42, 52, 59
Cycle of fifths (*see* Circle of fifths)

Direction, 17
Dominant order, 65
Dominant seventh, (*see* Chords)
Double pedal point, 162, 197, 253 (*see also* Organ point *and* Pedal point)
Double thirds (*see* Technique)
Duplet, 236

Embellishments, 73, 215–223
    afterbeat, 219
    appoggiatura, 216
    arpeggiated chords, 220
    grace note, long, 216
    grace note, short, 216
    gruppetto, 219
    inverted mordent, 216
    mordent, 216
    *pralltriller*, 216
    rolled chords, 220
    trill, full, 218
    trill, measured, 218
    turn, 221–223
Enharmonic relationship, 65, 110
Extended periods, 254 (*see* Improvisation)

Figured bass (*see* Bass)
Finger numbers, 2
Fingering:
    basic principles of, 24
    devices, 24
    inverted mordents, 218
    mirror, 178
    mordents, 218
    seventh chord arpeggios, 200
    standard scale, 110

Fingering (continued)
    in transposition, 66
    triad arpeggios, 147
    turns, 223
Five-finger position pattern, 3
Framing chords from above, 29
Framing chords at keyboard, 14
Framing octaves, 45, 249
Framing triads, 53
Fundamental position, 120 (*see also* Position, fundamental)

Graces (*see* Embellishments)
Ground bass (*see* Accompaniments)
Group Improvisation (*see* Improvisation)

Hand gymnastics, 10, 33, 46
Hand position, 4
Harmonizing melodies, 15, 27, 30, 43, 66, 92, 117, 122, 159, 184, 192–196, 224, 242–251
"Hunting up and Coursing down," 64 (*see also* Bell-ringing *and* Changes)

Improvisation, 20
    accompaniment patterns, new, 164
    accompaniments, broken-chord, 135
    for activities, 229
    boogie bass, 204
    on chord patterns, 201, 203
    with chromatic lower neighbors, 106
    composition techniques, using, 165
    in extended periods, 254
    given beginnings, continuing from, 37, 77, 106–107, 135–136, 164–165 (*see also* models)
    group, 20, 108
    "Indian Music," 253
    inversions, using, 164
    irregular phrases, 255
    melodic, 21
    models, 21, 22, 36, 58, 77, 106–107, 135–136, 164–165, 251 (*see also* given beginnings, continuing from)
    modulation in, 252
    non-harmonic tones, accented, 164
    with I and $V_7$, 36
    with I, IV, $V_7$ in major and minor modes, 58
    passing tones, unaccented, 77
    pentatonic scale, using, 107, 108
    resources, new, 252
    rhythmic, 21
    right-hand chords, 136
    sequences, 203–204, 251
    special effects, 252
    strumming, 204
    two–hand, 22
    two-piano, 204
"Inch worming," 94 (*see also* Octaves)
Interval, 1
    defined, 1
    identification, 89
    schedule, 89

Intervals, 1, 88
    augmented, 90
    compute, how to, 83
    diminished, 90
    doubly augmented, 90
    doubly diminished, 90
    half step, 1
    inverted, 89
    perfect, 89
Interpretation, basic principles of, 95
Introductions, 224
Inversions, seventh chord, 180
Inversions, triad, 84, 118, 152, 180
Irregular phrases, 255

Key, change of, 117, 252 (*see also* Modulation)
Key relationship, 186
Keyboard feel, 5, 14, 52
Keyboard sense (*see* Keyboard feel)
Kinesthetic approach to memorizing, 255

Leading tone, 62
    doubled, 184, 204
    rules governing, 184, 204
    tendency, 183
Ledger lines, recognizing, 75
Left-hand accompaniments (*see* Accompaniments)
Left-hand interest, 95, 122, 256

Melody in thirds and sixths (*see* Accompaniments)
Memorizing, 255
Memorizing, short-term, 125
Minor scales (*see* Scale fingering and Scale structure)
Mode, 40, 43, 82, 87
Models for improvisation (*see* Improvisation, models)
Modulation, 180, 186, 252
    basic formula, 186
    defined, 186
    diminished seventh, by means of the, 198 (*see also* Chords)
    dominant seventh, by means of the, 124, 186 (*see also* Chords)
    up one half step, 124, 188

Non-harmonic tones, 69
    accented, 164
    chromatic lower neighbor, 70, 106
    passing tones, accented, 70
    passing tones, unaccented, 70, 125

Octaves:
    framing (*see* Technique)
    "inch worming," 94
    names of, 46
    parallel, 154–155, 204
    playing, 44 (*see also* Technique)
Off beat (*see* Accompaniments)
Organ point, 162, 197 (*see also* Pedal point)
Ornaments (*see* Embellishments)

Parallel fifths, 154–155, 158, 204
Parallel minor scale, 81 (*see also* Scale structure, minor, tonic)
Parallel octaves, 154–155, 204
Part (*see* Voice)
Passing tones, accented (*see* Non-harmonic tones)
Passing tones, unaccented (*see* Non-harmonic tones)
Pattern (*see* Chord patterns)
Pedal:
    damper, 29, 56, 69, 129, 253
    in rhythm drills, 56, 69, 128
    soft, 130
    sostenuto, 130, 253
Pedal change, 131, 133
Pedal point, 162, 197, 253 (*see also* Organ point)
Pedaling:
    apparent inconsistencies in, 132
    basic principles of, 129–133
    direct, 130
    half-pedal, 133
    indications, 133
    legato (*see* syncopated)
    syncopated, 131
    trill, 133
    whole-tone scale, 132
Pentatonic (*see* Improvisation *and* Scale structure)
Phrase, 96
Phrasing, 96
Picardy third, 162
Playing by ear, 9
Plus sign, 81
Polytonality, 253
Position, fundamental, 120 (*see also* Root position)
Positions of triads, 84, 119


Related keys, 186
Relative major, 81, 117, 186
Relative minor, 40, 254
Replacement (*see* Fingering, sections on Standard Scale Fingering *and* Scale
    Chart in Appendix)
Rhythm, artificial, 236
Rhythm, habañera, 241
Rhythm drills, 10, 19, 34, 56, 69, 94, 128–129
    with pedal, 56, 69, 128–129
Root position, 119, 120
Roots:
    defined, 82
    rule for finding, 84
Round, A, 27


Scale-degree names, 62
Scale fingering: (*see also* Appendix)
    chromatic, 178
    diatonic, irregular, 177
    diatonic, standard, 110, 146, 177
    diatonic (major) in tetrachords, 60
    diatonic (minor) in tetrachords, 80
    mirror, 178
    rule for, 111
    whole-tone, 178

Scale structure:
    Byzantine, 253
    chromatic, 2
    diatonic, 3, 60, 80
    major, 60
    major, relative, 81, 117
    minor, 80
    minor, harmonic, 80, 82
    minor, melodic, 80
    minor, natural, 80, 82
    minor, parallel, 81
    minor, pure, 80, 82
    minor, tonic, 81
    pentatonic, 107
    whole-tone, 2

*Secondo* accompaniments (*see* Accompaniments)
Sequences, 203, 204, 214, 251
Sight-reading, 4, 17, 34, 51, 75, 105, 133, 162
    bass staff, 51
    with covered hands, 52
    factors in, 5, 17, 34, 52, 75, 133
    function of memory in, 34, 125
    interval shape recognition, 75
    ledger lines, 75
    linear direction, 17
    looking ahead, 5
    note-cluster (*see* note-group)
    note-group, 34
    pacer, 5
    preliminary survey, 5, 35
    stepwise and chordwise progression, 17
    two staves, 34

Singing tone, 96
Slur, function of, 31
Spelling, note, 65, 90, 124
Stepwise, 17
Strumming (*see* Accompaniments)
Subdominant order, 65
Subdominant tendency, 183


Technique:
    arpeggios, 147
    double thirds, 161, 212
    dynamic control, 127
    framing chords, 14, 29, 53, 243
    framing octaves, 44, 243, 249
    legato chords, 213
    legato repeated notes, 24, 213
    legato thirds, 161, 212
    octaves, 45
    relaxed wrist, 45
    repeated notes, 26, 93
    scales, 110, 146, 177 (*see also* Scale fingering)
    stretching, 126
    thumb flexibility, 150
    trill, 125, 218 (*see also* Embellishments)

*Tre corde*, 133
Triad (*see* Chords)
Triads in three positions, 84

Trills (*see* Technique, Embellishments, *and* Warmup XVI)
Triplet, 236

*Una corda*, 133

Voice (part), 15, 84, 85, 86, 87, 96, 117, 246, 247
Voice leading, 158, 198, 201, 246, 247
Voice movement, 85, 87  (*see also* Voice leading)

"We Want Ice Cream" (Figure 147), 157, 205